Nelson Monroe

The Grand army button

A souvenir

Nelson Monroe

The Grand army button
A souvenir

ISBN/EAN: 9783337221539

Printed in Europe, USA, Canada, Australia, Japan

Cover: Foto ©ninafisch / pixelio.de

More available books at **www.hansebooks.com**

THE

GRAND ARMY BUTTON

A SOUVENIR

DEDICATED TO "MY COMRADES," THE GRAND ARMY OF THE REPUBLIC
AND THE SONS OF VETERANS, OF THE UNITED STATES

BY

NELSON MONROE

REMINISCENCES OF THE DAYS OF DARK SECESSION
1861 AND 1865

———

"And we recognize this Button wheresoever it may be,
as a badge of glory won."

———

BOSTON
ROCKWELL AND CHURCHILL PRESS
1893

CONTENTS.

PREFACE.

THIS little book, which is presented to the public, is designed to keep the hearts of the people warm and grateful toward the noble defenders of the Union and freedom, who in so many weary and bloody struggles have upheld the nation's flag, the nation's honor, and the nation's life; of the life of our noble men whose trials and hardships in prisons and prison pens, and triumphs of the volunteer on many bloody fields of battle, whose immortal valor and patience have done the work and paid the price of liberty and peace.

Therefore,

" For what he was, and what he dared, remember him to-day."

THE GRAND ARMY BUTTON.

I HAVE seen a little button, of a copper-colored hue,
   It was worn upon the lapel of the boys who wore the blue;
It is made of cannon captured by the loyal, brave, and true,
               As they were marching on.

. . . .

Care for the soldier, who once cared for you,
Vet'ran and hero, the grand boy in blue;
Where would you now be, had not his brave life
Stood between you and the war's deadly strife ?
History's records forever will tell
Proudly the deeds of the heroes who fell,
Forcing rebellion and treason to cease,
Dying for liberty, union, and peace.

Humble in life though he may be to-day,
Little of wealth in his coffers may lay,
Riches are his, of more value than gold:
Valor displayed, passing all deeds of old.
You are his debtors for his gifts to you,
Show yourselves grateful, to justice be true.
Your safety he won, he won you your peace,
See that your blessings to him never cease.

Who are the worthiest the nation's true love ?
Who should be shielded till mustered above ?
'Tis but his due who imperilled his life;
Keep him from want, comfort children and wife.
Sacrifice grand for your safety he gave;
Bless him who suffered our country to save.

In the days of dark secession, sixty-one to sixty-five,
Not a star from off our banner could the haughty rebels rive.
Was the service in the army or upon the rolling sea,
It was the self-same struggle that has made the nation free;
And we recognize this button, wheresoever it may be,
               As a badge of glory won.

INTRODUCTION.

IN the early part of 1861, the true citizen heard that traitors at Washington had formed a conspiracy to overthrow the government, and, soon after, that the stars and stripes had been fired upon, and had been hauled down at the bidding of an armed enemy in South Carolina; that the capital of the nation was threatened; and that our new president had called for help. How quickly the citizen answered the call! Almost like magic he sprang forth a soldier.

His farm, his bench, his desk, his counter, were left behind, and you find him marching, through the then gloomy, flagless, defiant streets of Baltimore, fully equipped for service, with uniform gray, blue, red, or green, it then mattered not; with knapsack, cartridge-box, musket, and bayonet, his outfit was all that was required.

He was a little awkward, his accoutrements much awry, his will unsubdued.

He did not keep step to music, nor always lock step with his companions. He had scarcely ever fired a musket, but he had become a soldier, put on a soldier's garb, set his face toward the enemy, and, God willing, he purposed never to turn back till the soldier's work was done. You meet him at Washington — on Meridian Hill, perhaps; discipline and drill seize upon him, restrain his liberty, and mould his body. Colonels, captains, lieutenants, and sergeants, his former equals, order him about, and he must obey them. O what days, and O what nights! Where are home and affection? Where are the soft bed and the loaded table? Change of climate, change of food, want of rest, want of all kinds of old things, and an influx of all sorts of new things make him sick — yes, really sick in body and soul. But in spite of a few doses of quinine and a wholesome hospital bed and diet (as the soldier of '61 remembers them), his vigorous constitution and indomitable heart prevail, so that he is soon able to cross the Long Bridge and invade the sacred red clay of Virginia with his companions in arms.

Yet, perhaps, should you now observe him closely you will perceive his enthusiasm increasing faster even than his strength.

He is on the enemy's side of the river. Now for strict guard duty! Now for the lonely picket amid the thickets where men are killed by ambushed foes! How the eye and the ear and — may I say it? — the heart are quickened in these new and trying vigils! Before long, however, the soldier is inured to these things.

He becomes familiar with every stump, tree, and pathway of approach, and his trusty gun and stouter heart defy any secret foe.

Presently you find him on the road to battle. The hot weather of July, the usual load, the superadded twenty extra rounds of cartridges and three days' rations strung to his neck, and the long, weary march, quite exhaust his strength during the first day. He aches to leave the ranks and rest; but no, no! He did not leave home for the ignominious name of " straggler " and " skulker." Cost what it may, he toils on.

The Acotink, the Cub Run, the never-to-be-forgotten Bull Run, are passed. Here, of a sudden, strange and terrible sounds strike upon his ear and bear down upon his heart: the booming of shotted cannon; the screeching of bursted shell through the heated air, and the zip, zip, zip of smaller balls. Everything produces a singular effect upon him. Again, all at once, he is thrown quite unprepared upon a new and trying experience; for now he meets the groaning ambulance and the bloody stretcher.

He meets limping, armless, legless, disfigured, wounded men. To the right of him and to the left of him are the lifeless forms of the slain. Suddenly a large iron missile of death strikes close beside him and explodes, sending out twenty or more jagged fragments, which remorselessly maim or kill five or six of his mates before they have had the opportunity to strike one blow for their country. His face is now very pale; and will not the American soldier flinch and turn back? There is a stone wall, there is a building, there is a stack of hay. It is so easy to hide! But no! He will not be a coward. " O God, support and strengthen me! " 'Tis all his prayer. Soon he is at work. Yonder is the foe. " Load and fire! " " Load and fire! " But the cry comes, " Our flank is turned! " " Our men retreat! " With tears pouring down his cheek, he slowly yields and joins the retiring throng. Without any more nerve and little strength, he struggles back from a lost field. Now he drinks the dregs of suffering. Without blanket for the night, without food, without hope, it is no wonder that a panic seizes him, and he runs demoralized away. This disreputable course, however, is only temporary.

The soldier before long forgets his defeat and his sufferings, brightens up his armor, and resumes his place on the defensive line. He submits for weary days to discipline, drill, and hard fare; he wades through the snows of winter and the deep mud of a Virginia spring. He sleeps upon the ground, upon the deck of a transport steamer, and upon the floor of a platform car.

He helps load and unload stores; he makes facines and gabions; he corduroys quicksands and bridges, creeks and bogs. Night and day he digs or watches in the trenches. What a world of new experience! What peculiar labor and suffering he passes through the soldier alone can tell you. He now marches hurriedly to his second battle; soon after he is in a series of them. Fight and fall back; fight and fall back! O those days of hopelessness, sorrow, toil, and emaciation! How vividly the living soldier remembers them — those days when he cried from the bottom of his heart, "O God, how long! how long!"

Would you have patience to follow him through the commingling disasters, from the battle of Cedar Mountain to the same old Bull Run, you would emerge with him from the chaos and behold his glistening bayonet again on the successful field of Antietam, where a glimmer of hope lighted up his heart. Would you go with him to the bloody fields of Fredericksburg, stanch his wounds in the wilderness of Chancellorsville, and journey on with him afterward to this hallowed ground of Gettysburg, and could you be enabled to read and record his toils, his sufferings, and all his thoughts, you might be able to appreciate the true American soldier. You might then recite the first chapter of the cost of the preservation of the American Union. In September, 1863, after the battle of Gettysburg, the government sends two army corps to reinforce our brethren in the West. The soldier is already far from home and friends, but he is suddenly apprised that he must go two thousands miles farther. He cannot visit his family to take leave of them. He has scarcely the opportunity of writing a line of farewell. The chances of death are multitudinous as they appear before his imagination, and the hope of returning is very slender. Yet again the soldier does not falter. With forty others he crowds into the close unventilated freight-car, and speeds away, night and day, without even the luxury of a decent seat. With all the peculiar discomforts of this journey, the backings, and the waitings at the railroad junctions, the transfers from car to car and from train to train, being confined for days without the solace and strength derived from his coffee, there is yet something compensative in the exhilarating influence of change. And there is added to it, in passing through Ohio and Indiana, a renewed inspiration, as the people turn out in masses to welcome him and to bid him godspeed; and little girls throw wreaths of flowers round his neck, kiss his bronzed cheek, and strew his car with other offerings of love and devotion. Such impressions as were here received were never effaced. They touch the rough heart anew with tenderness, and, being a reminder of the old home affections, only serve to deepen his resolution sooner or later, by the blessing of God, to reach the goal of his ambition; that is to say, with his compatriots to secure to his children, and to other children, enduring peace, with liberty and an undivided country. He passes on through Kentucky, through the battlefields of Tennessee, already historical. The names Nashville, Stone River, Murfreesboro, and Tullahoma remind him of past struggles, and portend future conflicts. He is deposited at Bridgeport, Ala., a houseless, cheerless, chilly place on the banks of the Tennessee, possessing no interest further than that furnished by the railroad bridge destroyed and the yet remaining rubbish and filth of an enemy's camp. Before many days the soldier threads his way up the valley of the great river, which winds and twists amid the rugged mountains, till he finds himself beneath the rock-crowned steeps of Lookout. Flash after flash, volume after volume of light-colored smoke, and peal on peal of cannon, the crashing sound of shot and the screaming of shell, are the ominous signs of unfriendly welcome sent forth to meet him from this rocky height. Yet on he marches, in spite of threatening danger, in spite of the ambush along the route, until he has joined hands with his Western brother, who had come from Chattanooga to meet and to greet him. This is where the valley of Lookout joins that of the Tennessee. At this place the stories of Eastern and Western hardship, suffering, battling, and danger are recapitulated and made to blend into the common history and the common sacrifice of the American soldier.

Were there time, I would gladly take you, step by step, with the soldier, as he bridges and crosses the broad and the rapid river, as he ascends and storms the height of Mission Ridge, or as he plants his victorious feet, waves his banner, and flashes his gun on the top of Lookout Mountain. I would carry you with him across the death-bearing streams of Chickamauga. I would have you follow him in his weary, barefooted, wintry march to the relief of Knoxville and back to Chattanooga. From his point of view I would open up the spring campaign, where the great general initiated his remarkable work of genius and daring. I could point you to the soldier pursuing his enemy into the strongholds of Dalton, behind the stern, impassable features of Rocky Face. Resaca, Adairsville, Cassville, Dallas, New Hope Church, Pickett's Hill, Pine Top,

Lost Mountain, Kenesaw, Culps' Farm, Smyrna, Camp Ground, Peach Tree Creek, Atlanta, from so many points of view, and Jonesboro, are names of battle-fields upon each of which a soldier's memory dwells. For upward of a hundred days, he scarcely rested from the conflict. He skirmished over rocks, hills, and mountains; through mud, streams, and forests. For hundreds of miles he gave his aid to dig that endless chain of intrenchments which compassed every one of the enemy's fortified positions. He companied with those who combated the obstinate foe, on the front and on the flanks of those mountain fastnesses which the enemy had deemed impregnable, and he had a right at last to echo the sentiment of his indefatigable leader, " Atlanta is ours, and fairly won ! "

Could you now have patience to turn back with him and fight these battles over again, behold his communications cut, his railroad destroyed for miles and miles ; enter the bloody fight of Allatoona; follow him through the forced marches, *via* Rome, Ga., away back to Resaca, and through the obstructed gaps of the mountains of Alabama, — you would thank God for giving him a stout heart and an unflinching faith in a just and noble cause. Weary and worn, he reposes at Atlanta on his return but one single night, when he commences the memorable march toward Savannah. The soldier has become a veteran ; he can march all day with his musket, his knapsack, his cartridge-box, his haversack and canteen, upon his person ; his muscles have become large and rigid, so that what was once extremely difficult he now accomplishes with graceful ease. This fact must be borne in mind when studying the soldier's marches through Georgia and the Carolinas. The enemy burned every bridge across stream after stream ; the rivers bordered the swamps ; for example, the Ocmulgee, the Oconee, and the Ogeechee were defended at every crossing. That they were passed at all by our forces is due to the cheerful, fearless, indomitable private soldier. O that you had seen him, as I have done, wading creeks a half a mile in width, and water waist deep, under fire. pressing on through wide swamps, without one faltering step, charging in line upon the most formidable works, which were well defended. You could then appreciate him and what he has accomplished, as I do. You could then feel the poignant sorrow that I always did feel when I saw him fall bleeding to the earth.

I must now leave the soldier to tell his own tale among the people : of his bold, bloody work at McAllister against the torpedoes, abattis, artillery, and musketry ; of his privations at Savannah ; of his struggles through the swamps, quicksands, and over the broad rivers of the Carolinas ; of the fights, fires, explosions, doubts, and triumphs suggested by

Griswoldville, Rivers' and Binnaker's Bridges, Orangeburg, Congaree Creek, Columbia, Cheraw, Fayetteville, Averysboro, and Bentonville. I will leave him to tell how his hopes brightened at the reunion at Goldsboro; how his heart throbbed with gratitude and joy as the wires confirmed the rumored news of Lee's defeat, so soon to be followed by the capture of the enemy's capital and his entire army. I will leave him to tell to yourselves and your children how he felt and acted, how proud was his bearing, how elastic his step, as he marched in review before the President of the United States at Washington. I would do the soldier injustice not to say that there was one thing wanting to make his satisfaction complete, and that was the sight of the tall form of Abraham Lincoln, and the absence of that bitter recollection, which he could not altogether exclude from his heart, that he had died by the hand of a traitor assassin.

I have given you only glimpses of the American soldier as I have seen him. To feel the full force of what he has done and suffered, you should have accompanied him for the last four years; you should have stood upon the battle-fields during and after the struggle; and you should have completed your observation in the army hospitals, and upon the countless grounds peopled with the dead. The maimed bodies, the multitude of graves, the historic fields, the monumental stones, after all, are only meagre memorials of the soldier's work. God grant that what he planted, nourished, and has now preserved by his blood — I mean American liberty — may be a plant dear to us as the apple of the eye, and that its growth may not be hindered till its roots are firmly set in every State of this Union, and till the full fruition of its blessed fruit is realized by men of every name, color, and description in this broad land.

ABRAHAM LINCOLN.

A BRAHAM LINCOLN, sixteenth President of the United States, and at the time of his death filling that office for the second term, was born in Hardin County, Kentucky, Feb. 12, 1809. His ancestors were Quakers. In 1816 his father removed to Spencer County, Indiana, and Abraham was thus early put to work with an axe to clear away the forest. In the next ten years he received about one year's schooling, in such schools as were taught in that new country.

At the age of nineteen years he made a trip to New Orleans as a hired hand on a flat-boat. In March, 1830, he removed with his father to Decatur, Ill., and aided in building a cabin, settling the family in their new home, and providing for them the ensuing winter. In 1831 he again made a trip to New Orleans, and on his return became a clerk in a store at Sangamon, Ill.

In 1832 he volunteered in the Black Hawk War, and was made captain of a company, but saw no fighting. On his return from the campaign he was a candidate for the Legislature, but was unsuccessful. A store which he purchased did not prosper; and after a short term of service as postmaster at New Salem, Ill., studying at every leisure moment, he became a surveyor, and won a good reputation for the accuracy of his surveys.

In 1834 he was elected to the Legislature, and reëlected in 1836 and 1838. Having devoted all his leisure time to the study of law, he was admitted to the bar in 1836, and in 1837 removed to Springfield, Ill., and opened an office in partnership with Hon. John F. Stuart. He soon rose to eminence in his profession, but did not withdraw from politics. In 1844 he was nominated as a Whig presidential elector, and canvassed the State for Mr. Clay.

In 1846 he was elected to Congress from the central district of Illinois, and in Congress maintained the reputation of an honest and able representative, acting generally with the more advanced wing of the Whig party. In 1849 he was a candidate for United States Senator, but the Legislature was Democratic, and elected General Shields. In 1854 the passage of the Nebraska Bill and the repeal of the Missouri Compromise called him again into the field, and by his disinterested labors Judge Trumbull was elected to the United States Senate. In 1856, at the Republican National Convention, he was urged for the vice-presidency, and received one hundred and ten votes. In 1858 he was nominated for United States Senator by the Republicans, and in company with Judge Douglas, the Democratic candidate, canvassed the State, discussing with his antagonist the great principles which distinguished the two parties. Lincoln had a majority of the popular vote, but Douglas was elected by the Legislature by eight majority. On the 18th of May, 1860, Mr. Lincoln was nominated by the Republican National Convention at Chicago for the presidency, and on the 6th of February following was elected, receiving one hundred and eighty out of three hundred and three electoral votes. It was the policy of those who were conspiring against the Union to divide the opponents of Mr. Lincoln as far as possible, in order that he might succeed by the votes of Northern States alone, and thus afford a pretext for secession ; and therefore three other distinct presidential tickets were run, headed respectively by Messrs. Breckenridge, Douglas, and Bell.

As soon as his election was known, measures were taken by political leaders in several of the Southern States to drag their States into secession ; and when Mr. Lincoln left Springfield, Ill., on the 11th of February, to go to Washington for his inauguration, six States had already seceded, and others were preparing to follow. A Southern confederacy had been formed, with Davis and Stephens for president and vice-president. Notwithstanding three or more attempts to assassinate him, he reached Washington in safety, and, though still threatened, was inaugurated March 4, 1861. The condition of the government, through the imbecility, fraud, and treason of the preceding administration and cabinet, was deplorable : its credit nearly ruined ; its army deprived of arms and paroled ; its navy sent to distant seas ; its arms removed to the arsenals of the States in insurrection, or sold and broken up ; its forts, vessels, custom-houses, and mints seized by the conspirators.

Mr. Lincoln set himself to remedy this, when, on the 14th of April, 1861, Fort Sumter was captured and the war commenced. He then called for seventy-five thousand men for three months, proclaimed a blockade of the Southern ports, and summoned an extra session of Congress for July 4, 1861. Large armies were soon required, and in the executive responsibilities of his position in a time of war, with a great army to be maintained, disciplined, and kept at work, finances to be managed, the disloyal gov-

ernment officers, civil and military, to be weeded out, the schemes of
secessionists to be thwarted, and later in the year the difficult case of the
seizure of Mason and Slidell to be adjusted, he had his full share of the
burdens of his official position. During 1862, these were rather increased
than diminished.

Compelled by his convictions of duty to assume in fact his titular position of commander-in-chief of the army and navy, he ordered an advance in
February, 1862, which was made in March. The indecisive or disastrous
battles of the Peninsula and Pope's campaign caused him great anxiety,
and the conviction having been forced upon him, by the course of events,
that the slaves in the rebel States must be emancipated as a military
necessity, he issued, on the 22d of September, soon after the more favor-
able battles of South Mountain and Antietam, his preliminary proclamation, announcing his intention of declaring free all slaves in rebel States,
on the 1st of January, 1863. Several successes in the West had cheered
him, and in 1863, with some disasters, there were many and important
victories East and West. Mr. Lincoln had been very desirous that the
border States should adopt some plan of more or less gradual emancipation, and, during the year, West Virginia, Maryland, and Missouri did so.

In 1864, having called General Grant to the lieutenant-generalship, Mr.
Lincoln divided with him a part of his burdens, which had become too
oppressive to be borne. A great outcry had been made against him for
the arrest of Vallandigham and other promoters of rebellion ; but in two
very able letters, addressed to the New York and Ohio committees, he fully
justified his course.

The victories of Sherman, Thomas, Farragut, Terry, and Sheridan, and
the persistency and resolution of Grant, had at length, in the spring of
1865, prepared the way for the downfall of the rebellion ; and after a brief
but desperate struggle, Petersburg and Richmond fell, and Lee surrendered his army. In the progress of these events, Mr. Lincoln, whose
anxiety had been most insupportable, was at the front, and the day after
the occupation of Richmond by the Union troops he entered that city,
not with the pomp of a conqueror, but quietly and without display, and
after spending one day there returned to City Point, and thence to Washington. The war was to all intents and purposes closed, and, with his mind
intent on the great problem of pacification, his brow cleared, and he appeared in better spirits than usual. This was the time seized upon by the
conspirators for his assassination, and on the 15th of April, just four years
from the date of his proclamation calling the people to arms, he died by
the hand of a wretched murderer.

He was a man of thorough integrity and uprightness, conscientious, candid, amiable, and forgiving; slow in arriving at conclusions, but firm in maintaining them; of sound judgment and good executive abilities, and possessing a rare power of natural logic which was the more convincing from its singularity. Though sprung from the common people and never ashamed of the class, he possessed a native politeness and grace of manner which caused Edward Everett, himself one of the most refined and elegant gentlemen of our time, to say that in his personal bearing and manner Mr. Lincoln was the peer of any gentleman of America or Europe.

U. S. Grant

ULYSSES SIMPSON GRANT.

U LYSSES SIMPSON GRANT, Lieutenant-General, United States
Army, was born at Point Pleasant, Clermont County, O., April
27, 1822. After a fair preliminary education, he entered West
Point in 1839, and graduated in 1843, ranking twenty-first in a class of
thirty. Brevetted second lieutenant, Fourth Infantry, he served first at
Jefferson Barracks, near St. Louis; next on the Red River in Louisiana.
In 1845 made full second lieutenant in his regiment, and in 1846, under
General Taylor, moved forward to the border, took part in the battles of
Palo Alto, Reseca de la Palma, in the storming of Monterey and the
capture of Vera Cruz; appointed quartermaster of his regiment; took
part in the assault of Molinodel Rey and the storming of Chapultepec,
and was made first lieutenant on the spot and subsequently brevetted
captain. In August, 1848, married Miss Dent of St. Louis, and ordered
successively to Detroit, Sackett's Harbor, and Fort Dallas, Oregon.
Promoted to full captaincy in August, 1853; resigned his commission
July 31, 1854. He engaged in various occupations, but with no great
success, as farmer, collector, auctioneer, and leather-dealer. On the
opening of the war he raised a company and marched with it to Springfield, Ill., from Galena, his then residence. Other men of more imposing
appearance obtained commissions, but Captain Grant received none.
Soon after, however, Governor Gates made him adjutant-general, and in
June commissioned him as colonel of the Twenty-first Illinois Volunteers.
His regiment was employed in guarding the Hannibal and St. Joseph
Railroad. Here he was soon made acting brigadier-general, and on the
9th of August commissioned as brigadier-general and ordered to southern
Missouri to oppose Jefferson Thompson. He next took command of the
district of Cairo, occupied Paducah and Smithland, Ky., and sent an ex-
pedition in pursuit of Jefferson Thompson. On November 7 fought the
battle of Belmont. Early in January made a reconnoissance in force into
Kentucky to learn the position of the enemy, and in the beginning of
February moved on Fort Henry, Tenn., which, however, Flag-Officer
Foote captured before he reached it. He then besieged Fort Donelson,
on the Cumberland, and after four days received — Feb. 16, 1862 — its un-

conditional surrender. Promoted to a major-generalship Feb. 16, 1862.
Moving southward through Nashville, Franklin, Columbia, etc., he
reached Pittsburg Landing and Savannah, on the Tennessee River, the
latter part of March; fought the severe battle of Shiloh or Pittsburg
Landing April 6 and 7; under command of General Halleck took part
in the siege of Corinth. After its evacuation, put in command of the
Department of West Tennessee; broke up the illicit traffic at Memphis;
commanded in the battles of Iuka and Corinth September and October,
1862; moved southward to attack Vicksburg in rear, in December, 1862,
but was recalled by the capture of Holly Springs, his depot of supplies.
Returned northward, and bringing his army to Young's Point sought the
reduction of Vicksburg by various measures. Finally marching his force
down the west side of the river, crossed at Bruinsburg; fought in the
first seventeen days of May the battles of Fort Gibson, Fourteen Mile Run,
Raymond, Jackson, Champion's Hill, and Black River Bridge; besieged
Vicksburg for seven weeks, when it surrendered — by far the richest prize
of the war thus far; defeating and routing Johnston at Jackson with
Sherman's troops, he next visited New Orleans, where he was seriously
injured by being thrown from his horse.

Appointed in October, 1863, to the command of the Western Grand
Military Division, he hastened to Chattanooga, where by the magnificent
battles of Chattanooga he surpassed his previous reputation. He also
raised the siege of Knoxville. Appointed lieutenant-general in March,
1864, he reorganized the Eastern armies, and in May, 1864, commenced
his great campaign, and fought within the next weeks the terrible battles
of the Wilderness, Spottsylvania, Court House, the North Anna, Cold
Harbor, Mechanicsville, Chickahominy, and Petersburg; later in the
season, the disastrous battle of the Petersburg Mine, the battles of Deep
Bottom and Chaffin's Farm, several attempts to gain possession of the
South Side Railroad occasioning battles southwest of Petersburg, the
battles of Hatchers Run, in October, 1864, and February, 1865. The re-
pulse of the attack on Fort Stedman and the final movement by which
Five Forks was taken, and the strong works before Petersburg carried,
Richmond and Petersburg captured, the retreating rebel army pursued,
fought at Deatonville, Farmville, and Appomattox Station, and finally
compelled to surrender, demonstrated his ability and persistence. At the
same time he had directed in general the movements of Sherman, Sheridan, and Thomas, and in particular the expeditions for the capture of Fort
Fisher and the reduction of Wilmington. He also dictated the terms of
the subsequent surrender, and the reorganization of the greatly reduced
army.

WILLIAM TECUMSEH SHERMAN.

WILLIAM TECUMSEH SHERMAN, Major General, United States Army, was born in Lancaster, O., Feb. 8, 1820. After a good preliminary education he entered West Point in 1836, and graduated in 1840, sixth in his class ; appointed immediately second lieutenant Third Artillery, and served successively in Florida (where, in 1841, he was promoted to be first lieutenant), Fort Moulton (1841-6), in California (1846-50), where he was made assistant adjutant-general, brevetted captain, and in 1850 promoted to a captaincy, and ordered to St. Louis. In 1851 he was stationed at New Orleans. In 1853 he resigned his commission, removed to San Francisco, and was for four years manager of Lucas Turner & Co.'s banking-house. In 1857 he was offered the presidency of a State military academy in Louisiana, and accepted, but resigned in January, 1861, because the academy was used to train rebel officers, and removed to St. Louis, and at the opening of the war offered his services to the government. He was appointed, May 14, 1861, colonel of the Thirteenth Infantry, United States Army, and commanded the Third Brigade in the First (Tyler's) Division at Bull Run, where neither he nor his men ran, but rendered efficient service. He was made brigadier-general of volunteers Aug. 3, 1861, reported at first to General Anderson, and on General Anderson's resigning (October 8) was made commander of the Department of the Ohio. Here he was greatly embarrassed by the utter insufficiency of the force allowed him to meet the rebels, who greatly outnumbered his forces. Finding remonstrances useless, he asked to be relieved, and was shelved by being put in command of Benton Barracks near St. Louis. General Halleck found him here, and presently put him in command of the Fifth Division of Grant's Army. At Shiloh General Grant testifies that he saved the army and the day. He was in the advance in the pursuit and siege of Corinth, and was made major-general of volunteers from May 1, 1862. June 20 he captured Holly Springs, Miss. In June he was put in command of the district of Memphis, and suppressed the contraband trade and the guerrillas there. In December he was appointed to the command of the Fifteenth Army Corps, and sent to Chickasaw Bluffs, Vicksburg, where, owing to Grant's inability to coöperate, in consequence of the capture of Holly Springs by the rebels, he was repulsed with considerable loss. He then proceeded with his command and General McClunand, who ranked him to Arkansas Post, which was captured early in January, 1863. In Grant's subsequent campaign against Vicksburg, Sherman was his ablest lieutenant. He saved the gunboats from destruction on the Sunflower River, made so formidable a demonstration against Haines's Bluff, when Grant was at Bruinsburg, as to completely deceive the rebels and draw them away from his route; fought bravely at Fourteen Mile Creek and Jackson, destroyed rebel property there, and thence moved rapidly toward Vicksburg; captured the rebel batteries on Haines, Walnut, Snyder, and Chickasaw Bluffs, and then opened communication with the Union fleet above Vicksburg. He assaulted the city on the 19th and 22d of May, and gained some ground, though he did not enter the city. Immediately after the surrender in July, he was sent in pursuit of Johnston, whom he drove back through and out of Jackson with heavy loss.

After a short period of rest, he was called to reinforce the Army of the Cumberland at Chattanooga, and while on his way was put in command of the Army of the Tennessee, General Grant, who had formerly commanded it, being promoted to the command of the Military Division of the Mississippi. Arriving at Chattanooga, he was at once ordered to move to the attack of the rebels at the northern extremity of Missouri Bridge. He crossed the Tennessee, and, by his persistent demonstrations on Fort Buckner, compelled the rebels to withdraw their troops from Fort Bragg to oppose him, and then that fort fell a prey to the assault of the Fourth Corps. This battle over, he was immediately sent by General Grant to raise the siege of Knoxville, which he accomplished by an extraordinary forced march. After a brief period of rest, early in February General Sherman was at Vicksburg, at the head of twenty thousand troops, marching into the heart of Mississippi and Alabama. On his return Grant was lieutenant-general, and Sherman again succeeded him in the command of the Military Division of the Mississippi. Gathering his troops, he moved from Chattanooga May 7, 1864, for Atlanta, capturing in the campaign Dalton, Resaca, Kingston, Rome, Dallas, Allatoona Pass, Marietta, Sandtown, and Decatur, besides many places of less note, and fighting the severe battles of Rocky-Faced Ridge, Resaca, New Hope Church, Dallas, Kenesaw Mountain, Little Kenesaw, the three battles before Atlanta, and the battles at Jonesboro. He entered Atlanta September 1,

WILLIAM TECUMSEH SHERMAN.

removed the civilians from it, and gathered stores there; and Hood, the rebel general, attempting to cut his communications, he followed him northward, fought him at Allatoona Pass, drove him westward to Gaylesville, Ala., and intrusted the task of taking care of him to General Thomas while he returned to Atlanta, voluntarily severed all communication with Chattanooga, destroyed the public buildings of Atlanta, and with a force of sixty thousand men commenced his march toward Savannah Sweeping through a broad tract, he arrived at Savannah with very slight loss, capturing Fort McAllister by assault, and compelling Hardee to evacuate the city. He remained there a month, recruiting and setting matters in order, and with a force of nearly eighty thousand moved northward toward Goldsboro, N.C. On his route he captured Orangeburg, Columbia, and Winnsboro, S.C., compelled the rebels to evacuate Charleston, took Cheraw and Fayetteville, and entered Goldsboro on the 24th of March, having fought two battles at Averysboro and Bentonville, the latter one of considerable severity. Remaining seventeen days at Goldsboro to reclothe and refit his army, he moved, April 10, on Smithfield, and thence to Raleigh and westward. Receiving overtures for surrender from Johnston, he made a memorandum of an agreement with him, which, being unsatisfactory to the government, was annulled, and on the 26th of April Johnston surrendered on the same terms on which Lee had done.

The war ended, General Sherman was put at the head of one of the five great military divisions, that of the Mississippi, embracing the Northwestern States and territories, Missouri, and Arkansas.

PHILIP HENRY SHERIDAN.

PHILIP HENRY SHERIDAN, Major-General, United States Army, was born in Perry County, Ohio, in 1831. He had the advantages of a good common-school education, and was appointed to a cadetship at West Point in 1848, and graduated in 1853, very low in his class, his belligerent disposition reducing his standing in his studies, which was otherwise above the average.

He was attached to the First United States Infantry as a brevet second lieutenant, and ordered to Fort Duncan, Texas. In the spring of 1855 he was transferred to the Fourth Infantry as full second lieutenant, and ordered to San Francisco, *via* New York. In the latter city, he was for two months in command of Fort Wood. For six months he remained on the Pacific coast, and among the Indian tribes, whose confidence he had won, and whom he could manage better than any other officer.

He was promoted to a first lieutenancy in the winter of 1861, and when the war broke out, to a captaincy in the Thirteenth Infantry, United States Army, and ordered to join his regiment at Jefferson Barracks, near St. Louis. He was made acting chief quartermaster under General Custis, but succeeded indifferently. During the Pea Ridge campaign, he was ordered by General Blunt to impress a large amount of provender from the citizens of Arkansas, and, refusing, was put under arrest, and ordered to report to General Halleck, who relieved him from arrest, made him his own chief quartermaster, and presently allowed him to accept a commission of colonel of a Michigan cavalry regiment.

On the 14th of July, 1862, with his regiment, he fought and defeated a rebel brigade of cavalry, for which he was made brigadier-general of volunteers, his commission dating from July 1, 1862; but his command was infantry, not cavalry, to which he was best adapted.

Not to speak of some Union engagements in which Sheridan acquitted himself well, he held the key of the Union position at Perryville October 8, and saved the Union Army from defeat. In the battle of Stone River his division fought with the utmost desperation, losing all the brigade commanders, seventy officers, and half the men, and finally fell back in good order with empty cartridge-boxes, but, reforming, fought through the remaining days of the battle. At Chickamauga, on the first day, he prevented a serious disaster to Wood's corps; and on the second day, though driven from the field by the sudden assault of the enemy upon the gap in the Union lines, he fought his way out, and, reforming his men, brought his division into line before midnight.

At Chattanooga, his bravery and daring were conspicuous in the attack upon Fort Bragg. His horse was shot under him, and the men under his leadership were almost frantic with excitement. He followed Sherman to Knoxville, to raise the siege of that city; and when General Grant became lieutenant-general, he was ordered to the Army of the Potomac, to the command of the Cavalry Corps. In this congenial position he led several expeditions into the enemy's country, where he manifested the utmost daring and skill.

In August, at General Grant's request, he was appointed to the command of the Middle Military Division. Here he had for his task the keeping of the rebel General Early in order. After several minor skirmishes, he defeated him severely on the 19th of September, near Winchester; again on the 22d at Fisher's Hill; routed and drove him back on the 8th and 12th of October; and on the 19th of October, at Middletown, turned what had been, in his absence, a sad and disastrous defeat of his troops into a magnificent victory. In the next three or four months he desolated the Shenandoah Valley and smaller valleys adjacent, that they might no longer serve as harboring-places for guerrillas; and in March, 1865, descended the valley, captured Staunton and Waynesboro, routed Early once more, and destroyed the railroads and canals and other property, to the value of over fifty millions of dollars. Marching by way of White House, he joined General Grant's army, and after two days' rest was ordered to the field in the last campaign, where to his bravery and strategic skill was mainly due the capture of Five Forks and the pursuit and eventual surrender of Lee.

After the war on the Atlantic coast was over, he was sent, in command of a force of over eighty thousand men, to Texas; and Kirby Smith having surrendered, after a few weeks' guarding of the border he was allowed to reduce his army. On the 27th of June he was appointed commander of the Military Division of the Gulf, comprising the department of Mississippi, Louisiana, Texas, and Florida.

In 1869 General Sheridan was promoted to lieutenant-general, vice Sherman, promoted to the rank of general, positions which both these soldiers filled entirely to the satisfaction of the whole country.

PHILIP HENRY SHERIDAN.

LEE'S SURRENDER,

AT

APPOMATTOX COURT HOUSE, VIRGINIA, APRIL 9, 1865.

—·—

ABOUT April 1, 1865, the confederate forces under General Lee were totally routed and flying before Grant's army; victory and peace seemed very near, and General Grant wrote the following letter to Lee :

FARMVILLE, VA., April 7, 1865.

GENERAL : The results of the last week must convince you of the hopelessness of further resistance on the part of the army of northern Virginia in this struggle. I feel that it is so, and regard it as my duty to shift from myself the responsibility of any further effusion of blood, by asking of you the surrender of that portion of the Confederate States Army known as the army of northern Virginia.

U. S. GRANT,
Lieutenant-general.

Lee had been counseled by his own officers to surrender. He hesitated to acquiesce in their advice, saying, "I have too many brave men. The time has not yet come to surrender." Still he replied to Grant's letter on the evening of the same day :

GENERAL : I have received your note of this day. Though not entirely of the opinion you express of the hopelessness of further resistance on the part of the army of northern Virginia, I appreciate your desire to avoid useless effusion of blood, and therefore, before considering your proposition, ask the terms you will offer on condition of the surrender.

GEN. R. E. LEE.

Gibbon Custer. Babcock. Marshall Taylor Sheridan. Rawlins. Griffin Meade Parker. Forsyth. Bowers. Ord
          Comstock.   R. E. LEE.   U. S. GRANT.   Merritt.

THE SURRENDER OF GEN. R. E. LEE TO GEN. U. S. GRANT AT APPOMATTOX C. H., VA., APRIL 9, 1865.

This note was placed in General Grant's hands on the morning of the 8th, while he was still at Farmville. He immediately replied:

GENERAL: Your note of last evening in reply to mine of the same date, asking the conditions on which I will accept the surrender of the army of northern Virginia, is just received. In reply I would say that, peace being my great desire, there is but one condition I would insist upon: namely, that the men and officers surrendered shall be disqualified for taking up arms against the government of the United States until properly exchanged. I will meet you, or will designate officers to meet any officers you may name for the same purpose, at any point agreeable to you, for the purpose of arranging definitely the terms upon which the surrender of the army of northern Virginia will be received.

U. S. GRANT,
Lieutenant-general.

Meanwhile the Union army kept on in its pursuit, and the fighting continued. Early on the 8th, Grant set out from Farmville to join Sheridan's advance. He had been absent from his own headquarters several days, and, worn out with anxiety and fatigue, loss of sleep, and the weight of responsibility, he became very unwell, and was obliged to halt at a farmhouse on the road. While here he received about midnight another letter from Lee.

APRIL 8.

I received at a late hour your note to-day. In mine of yesterday I did not intend to propose the surrender of the army of northern Virginia, but to ask the terms of your proposition. To be frank, I do not think the emergency has arisen to call for the surrender of this army, but as the restoration of peace should be the sole object of all, I desired to know whether your proposals would lead to that end. I cannot, therefore, meet you with a view to surrender the army of northern Virginia; but as far as your proposal may affect the Confederate States forces under my command, I should be pleased to meet you at 10 A.M. to-morrow on the old stage-road to Richmond, between the picket lines of the two armies.

R. E. LEE.

This letter was thoroughly disingenuous and unworthy of Lee. On the other hand, Grant in reply used direct language and meant what he said. He wrote, on the morning of the 9th of April:

GENERAL: Your note of yesterday is received. I have no authority to treat on the subject of peace. The meeting proposed at 10 A.M. to-day could lead to no good. I will state, however, that I am equally desirous for peace with yourself, and the whole North entertains the same feeling. The terms upon which peace can be had are well understood. By the South laying down their arms, they would hasten that most desirable event, save thousands of human lives, and hundreds of millions of property not yet destroyed. Seriously hoping that all our difficulties may be settled without the loss of another life, I subscribe myself, etc.

U. S. GRANT,
Lieutenant-general.

Lee received Grant's letter on the morning of the 9th, and at once replied:

GENERAL: I received your note of this morning on the picket line, whither I had come to meet you, and ascertain definitely what terms were embraced in your proposal of yesterday with reference to the surrender of this army. I now ask an interview, in accordance with the offer contained in your letter of yesterday, for that purpose.

R. E. LEE.

This communication did not reach Grant until about noon. He immediately returned answer:

GENERAL: Your note of this date is but this moment (11.50 A.M.) received, in consequence of my having passed from the Richmond and Lynchburgh roads to the Farmville and Lynchburgh road. I am at this writing about four miles west of Walkin Church, and will push forward to the front for the purpose of meeting you. Notice sent to me on this road where you wish the interview to take place will meet me.

U. S. GRANT.

On receipt of this note Lee rode to the village of Appomattox, and selected the house of a farmer named McLean for his interview with Grant. Grant having received information of Lee's waiting at the farm-house, at once proceeded to the interview. The house was a very plain building, with a verandah. Grant was conducted through a narrow hall into a small parlor containing a centre table, one or two small stands, a sofa, and two or three chairs. Lee was accompanied by his military secretary and chief-of-staff, Col. Charles Marshall. The two great commanders shook hands heartily, and had scarcely taken their seats when their first words were interrupted by the entrance of the Union officers.

General Grant had not personally met General Lee since the two were in Mexico together, the latter then on the staff of Scott, the former a subaltern. The conversation naturally hinged at first upon these old recollections. Then there was a slight pause, which was broken by General Lee, who said: " I asked to see you, general, to find out upon what terms you would receive the surrender of my army."

General Grant thought a moment and replied: " My terms are these: All officers and men must become prisoners of war, giving up, of course, all weapons, munitions, and supplies. But a parole will be accepted, binding officers and men to go to their homes and remain there until exchanged, or released by proper authority."

Lee responded to this with a remark not exactly pertinent to the occasion; whereupon Grant continued, asking:

" Do I understand, General Lee, that you accept these terms? "

" Yes," replied Lee, faltering. " If you will put them in writing, I will put my signature to them."

General Grant, without saying more, again took seat at the table, and wrote the following:

APPOMATTOX COURT HOUSE,

VIRGINIA, April 9, 1865.

GENERAL: In accordance with the substance of my letter to you of the 8th inst., I propose to receive the surrender of the army of northern Virginia on the following terms, to wit: Rolls of all the officers and men to be made in duplicate, one copy to be given to an officer to be designated by me, the other to be retained by such officer or officers as you may designate. The officers to give their individual paroles not to take up arms against the government of the United States until properly exchanged, and each company or regimental commander to sign a like parole for the men of their commands. The arms, artillery, and public property to be parked and stacked, and turned over to the officers appointed by me to receive them. This will not embrace the side arms of the officers, nor their private horses or baggage. This done, each officer and man will be allowed to return to his home, not to be disturbed by the United States authorities so long as they observe their paroles and the laws in force where they may reside.

U. S. GRANT,
Lieutenant-general.

While Grant was penning these words he chanced to look up, and his eyes fell upon General Lee's sword. He paused for a moment, his mind conceived a new thought, and he inserted in the document the provision that "This will not embrace the side arms of the officers, nor their private horses or baggage."

General Lee read what Grant had written. He was touched by the clemency of the victorious commander, and on laying down the paper said simply, in a husky tone of voice, "Magnanimous, general." But he essayed to gain a few points, and remarked: "The horses of my cavalry and artillery, general, are the property of the soldiers. It is, I hope, within the terms that they shall retain their property."

" It is not within the terms," replied General Grant.

Lee glanced at the paper again and then said, "No. You are right. The terms do not allow it."

" And now," said Grant, " I believe the war is over, and that the surrender of this army will be followed soon by that of all the others. I know that the men, and, indeed, the whole South, are impoverished. I will not change the terms of the surrender, General Lee, but I will instruct my officers who receive the paroles to allow the cavalry and artillery to retain their horses, and take them home to work their little farms."

" Such an act on your part, general," replied Lee, " will have the best effect in the South."

He then sat down and wrote out the following letter :

HEADQUARTERS ARMY OF NORTHERN VIRGINIA,
April 9, 1865.

GENERAL: I received your letter of this date containing the terms of the surrender of the army of northern Virginia as proposed by you. As they are substantially the same as those expressed in your letter of the 8th inst , they are accepted. I will proceed to designate the proper officers to carry the stipulations into effect.

R. E. LEE,
General.

LIEUT.-GEN. U. S. GRANT.

General Grant returned to his headquarters, where the firing of salutes welcomed him. He gave orders to have it stopped at once.

" The war is over," he said; " the rebels are our countrymen again, and the best sign of rejoicing will be to abstain from all demonstrations in the field."

He dismounted by the roadside, sat down on a stone, and called for pencil and paper. An aide-de-camp offered him his order book, taking which, he wrote:

HON. E. M. STANTON, *Secretary of War, Washington :*

General Lee surrendered the army of northern Virginia this afternoon, on terms proposed by myself. The accompanying additional correspondence will show the condition fully.

U. S. GRANT,
Lieutenant-general.

And thus Grant announced to the government the end of the great rebellion.

FROM THE WAR DEPARTMENT,
WASHINGTON, D.C., April 9, 1865.

LIEUTENANT-GENERAL GRANT: Thanks be to Almighty God for the great victory with which He has this day crowned you and the gallant armies under your command. The thanks of this department, and of the government and of the people of the United States, their reverence and honor, have been deserved, and will be rendered to you and the brave and gallant officers and soldiers of your army, for all time.

EDWIN M. STANTON,
Secretary of War.

And thus with the surrender of Gen. Robert E. Lee, commander of the Confederate Army, to Gen. Ulysses S. Grant, commander of the United States Army, came the end of this unholy rebellion.

REVIEW OF THE WAR.

THE war which commenced in the spring of 1861, and was maintained for four years with a violence and intensity hardly equalled in modern history, was not, on the part of the South, a sudden uprising, the resilience of a brave and generous people, goaded at last to resistance after years of oppression and wrong, and without previous preparation seizing on such weapons as were available to throw off the hated yoke. On the contrary, it was but the fulfilment of a long-cherished purpose. Thirty years before, South Carolina had revolted; and though partly coaxed and partly awed into submission at that time, the political leaders of that and other Southern States had never ceased to threaten secession whenever their demands had been refused in the National Legislature; and from the presidential campaign of 1856 they had made active preparations to consummate their purpose at the next presidential election.

In the cabinet of Mr. Buchanan they had their pliant tools to furnish from the nation's resources the means of destroying the nation's life; and while one had quietly sent to the States which were to rise in rebellion the arms and ammunition intended for the nation's defence, till seven hundred and seven thousand stand of arms had been placed in the Southern arsenals, another had sent all the ships of the navy, except a mere handful, to distant seas for long cruises, and another had so depreciated the credit of the Republic that its bonds, which in 1857 stood at a premium of seventeen per cent., had, in a time of profound peace, fallen to eighty-five per cent., and even at this price no large sums could be placed. The Indian agencies had been given over to plunderers until the natives were exasperated and ready to rise and massacre the whites. Abroad, several of the more important missions and consulships were filled by men hostile to the nation's existence. And in the army and navy all the officers from the South and many of those from the North had been tampered with, and urged by the strongest inducements to abandon the cause of their country. What, then, were the causes which led to the rebellion? They were mainly:

1. An entire difference of opinion in regard to the fundamental principles of government, arising from the different social and economical conditions of society North and South. The men of the North were the descendants, for the most part, of the middle class of English yeomen. Sturdy, self-reliant, not averse to labor, but enterprising and intelligent, they had maintained commerce, established manufactories, fostered the mechanic arts, and developed, by high and scientific culture, the agricultural wealth of their region. They had organized free schools over their entire territory; reared academies, colleges, and universities of the highest character, and planted their churches over the entire region. With them labor was honorable, and the hard hand of the son of toil more welcome than the lily fingers of the children of indolence. The men of the South were descended in almost equal numbers from the profligate and vicious younger sons of the English aristocracy of two centuries ago and the convicts who were sent over, to the number of more than a hundred thousand while Virginia and Maryland were penal colonies, with a small infusion of Huguenots in South Carolina, and a considerable number of French creoles in Louisiana. Naturally averse to labor, they had, early in their history, commenced the importation of African slaves, and, under the stimulus of the profit to be derived from the culture of cotton, had laid out the Southern States in large plantations, often of many thousand acres, which were cultivated by slave labor, while the proprietors of the plantations and slaves led an easy and luxurious life. There was little commerce, and of that little nineteen-twentieths was conducted by Northern men. The manufactures were very few, and, for the most part, only of the rudest kind — coarse burlaps, negro cloth, the simpler agricultural implements, etc., while the great bulk of needful articles, either for war or peace, were brought from the North. The mechanic arts did not flourish, for it was not respectable to be a mechanic. Agriculture on an extended scale, though prosecuted with the rudest implements and in the most slovenly manner, was the only avocation which was popular; and at this the slaves were, except in the mountainous districts, the only toilers. All the whites were not planters, and as most of those who possessed neither plantations nor slaves were in abject poverty, and the system of large plantations rendered good free schools impossible, there grew up a class of poor, degraded whites, ignorant, depraved, and vicious, hating the negro intensely, and often inferior to him in intelligence. The slave system of agriculture was proverbially wasteful and destructive; and the rich and fertile lands of the South, after a few years of the reckless and superficial cultivation bestowed upon them, became barren, and the slaveholders emigrated to newer lands

to ruin them in the same way. There was thus a constant demand for new territory, to be sacrificed to the slave-holders; and as the large planters were often men of intelligence, and resolute in their defence of the principles of their caste, and could readily obtain seats in Congress, they were determined to secure for themselves and their fellow-planters the right of taking their slaves to any portion of the new territories, and bringing them under the influence of slavery.

2. The State Rights doctrine, first broached by Thomas Jefferson and James Madison in 1798, amplified and enlarged by John C. Calhoun in 1832 and 1833, and finally fully adopted by the principal Southern leaders between 1850 and 1860, was another cause of the rebellion. The advocates of this doctrine insisted upon the supremacy of the State in all matters. The Union was, they said, only a confederation of States, with but feeble powers, and when the sovereign States saw fit to secede from it they had a perfect right to do so. This right was to be exercised whenever the majority in Congress or the States should adopt any measure by which a sovereign State should feel or fancy itself aggrieved.

3. But slavery, directly or indirectly, was the proximate cause of the war. The North, with its regard for free and honorable labor, felt an abhorrence for slavery; and the poor bondman flying from its torments, its indignities, and its vicious indulgence was reluctantly sent back into its vortex, and often succeeded in effecting his escape. To sacrifice to such a system the virgin soil of the new territories seemed a crime against nature, and claiming an equal right to the fair lands, as yet unsettled, with the South, the citizens of the North refused to sanction slavery in any region beyond that already yielded by past compromises. On the other hand, the Southern leaders, accustomed to control Congress by their demands or threats, sought the permission to make slave territory of all the region west of Missouri, the recovery of their slaves everywhere in the United States, and the right to take them where they pleased without incurring risk of loss. They claimed also the right of reopening the slave-trade, and of maintaining the interstate slave-trade.

They saw, however, with serious apprehension, that in each successive Congress their power, hitherto enforced by haughty threats and the crack of the slave-driver's whip, was waning, as new Western States were admitted, and the opposition to slavery and slave-holding aggression became stronger and more effectually organized. In 1856 this opposition first excited their alarm. John C. Fremont, the candidate of the Republican Party for president, and the representative of the men who were hostile to any farther aggressions of the slave power, polled a very heavy vote ; and, though defeated, his party evidently possessed strength enough to succeed next time.

The slave-holding leaders at once took measures, quietly, to thwart such a result if it should happen. Many of them were not averse to a disruption of the Union, if only they might make suitable preparation for it beforehand ; and while, as we have said, the cabinet of Mr. Buchanan lent themselves willingly to the plans of the conspirators, measures were taken in other quarters to provide for the coming emergency. Military schools for the training of officers were established in many of the Southern States, and superintended by eminent graduates of West Point ; South Carolina imported large quantities of arms and munitions of war from England. The railroads and telegraph lines through the South, built mostly with Northern capital, were pushed forward with great rapidity ; and at length, so confident were the arch conspirators of success, and that with but moderate resistance, that they purposely incited divisions in the Democratic party, and other opponents of the Republican party, which, by the nomination of three other candidates for the presidency, should insure the success of the Republican nominee. This accomplished, their orators, by the most vehement denunciation of Mr. Lincoln and the North, sought to " fire the Southern heart " and prepare the excitable masses for the tragedy of secession. The people of the North, meantime, except those who were in the secret of the conspirators, sturdily refused to believe that the South intended to secede or fight. They had so often heard threats of secession from Southern leaders that the cry of " Wolf! Wolf! " had lost its terrors. The day of election came, and Mr. Lincoln was elected by a large majority of the electoral college and a plurality of the popular vote. Within four days after the election, South Carolina had called a secession convention, and on the 17th of December passed an ordinance of secession ; Mississippi imitated her example on the 9th of January ; Florida on the 10th ; Alabama on the 11th ; Georgia on the 19th ; and Louisiana on the 25th ; while Texas followed on the 7th of February. The election of Mr. Lincoln was the occasion, but in no sense the cause, of secession. Seven of the seceding States had passed the ordinance before he had left his home in Illinois to come to Washington to take the oath of office. The Senate and the Supreme Court of the United States were both opposed to him politically, and the House had but a small majority in his favor. There were not wanting those who hoped that by yielding to the demands of the Southern leaders, making concessions and compromises as in the past, war might yet be averted, and the " erring sisters come back in peace." A peace conference was accordingly assembled in Washington on the 4th of February, 1861. Delegates were present from twenty States, and various measures were discussed. A majority finally united in a series of propositions which gave no satisfaction to any party, and were rejected by both.

Mr. Crittenden offered in Congress a series of compromise resolutions, which after long discussion and numerous modifications were finally rejected. At this juncture one of the leading conspirators, afterward president of the rebel confederacy, avowed that no propositions could be made which would be satisfactory to them; that if offered *carte-blanche* to write their demands they would refuse it, as they were determined upon separation.

Mr. Lincoln was inaugurated; and before he and his cabinet had fairly learned the condition of the nation the conspirators precipitated the war upon the government. There was now no possibility of compromise or settlement. The war must be fought out till one or the other party should be ready to yield. How stood at this time the two opposing parties, the United States and the insurgents, as to their preparation for the conflict? The conspirators had thirty thousand men already under arms, and a hundred thousand more already called out and fast organizing for service. They had a moiety of the living graduates of West Point ready to take command of their armies, and the graduates of their half-dozen military schools for subordinate officers; they had an ample supply of muskets and rifles and pistols from the United States armories, furnished by the fraud and treason of John B. Floyd; and a large supply of cannon of all calibres in the arsenals, forts, and navy yards they had seized. The people, wrought up to frenzy by the harangues of the conspirators enlisted with great promptness; and there was reason to fear that they would seize upon the capital and wreck the government before the slower North could put on its harness for the fight.

But besides these advantages they had others of no mean importance. From the first it was evident that their fighting would, for the most part, be defensive, though with offensive returns. Adopting this mode of warfare, they reserved to themselves the great advantage of interior lines; that is, supposing the two armies to occupy in their positions segments of two parallel circles, the outer segment and what was *beyond* it would represent the position of the union army, while the inner segment and what was within it would exhibit the position of the rebel army. Of course troops, supplies, arms, and ammunition could be moved much more readily across the area included within the inner segment than around the outer one.

without discipline, except in the case of a very few regiments. The men, in many instances never having handled a musket before their enlistment, were hardly arrived in their camps before a cry was set up by the newspapers of, "On to Richmond!" and the fiercest denunciations were heaped upon the administration and the veteran lieutenant-general because he did not order an immediate advance. Meantime, though all possible expedition had been used, the regiments had hardly been formed into brigades, or the brigades into divisions. There was much to be learned in five or six weeks; but the clamor arose so fiercely, "On to Richmond! On to Richmond!" that General Scott suffered himself to be over-persuaded, and ordered an advance when the troops were as yet wholly unprepared for it, though some of them were approaching the close of their very short term of enlistment. Then followed the battle of Bull Run. It is much to the credit of this undisciplined mass of militia that they should have fought so well as they did. The far better trained force of Beauregard was beaten back, and, but for the arrival of Johnston's reinforcements just at the last moment, would have given way, routed and utterly discomfited. But the evil effects of the want of discipline showed themselves in the panic which affected the Union troops when their reinforced foe began to rally and press them back. But not all mingled in this terrible panic; a few regiments maintained their ground, and found that the rebels were too much exhausted and had suffered too heavy losses to assume the offensive.

The day seemed one of sad disaster, but it was a blessing in disguise. Rallying promptly from its deep humiliation, the nation saw the need of thorough discipline, of able leadership, of skilful strategy. Had the North been successful at Bull Run, the war would not yet be ended. After this battle, General McClellan, who had already won some distinction in West Virginia, became the actual, and in November following the titular, general-in-chief of the armies of the Union. At the West there were some movements worthy of notice. Captain Lyon, U.S.A., soon after brigadier-general of volunteers, held command in Missouri, where the governor, Claiborne F. Jackson, and Sterling Price, a former governor and then major-general of the Missouri State Guard and president of the State Convention, were endeavoring to compel the secession of the States.

Removing the United States arms from St. Louis, and arresting a brigade of the State Guard under General Frost, who sought to seize St. Louis in the interests of the secessionists, General Lyon soon compelled Jackson, Price, and their adherents to fly westward, driving them from the capital, skirmishing with them at Booneville, and finally pushing them to a point where the rebel general, McCulloch, brought up his forces to aid them. He fought and defeated them at Dug Spring on the 2d of August, 1861, and on the 9th of the same month, in the desperate and hard-fought battle of Wilson's Creek, he fell while leading his troops in a charge upon the enemy. His death temporarily disheartened his troops, who retreated to Rolla. A few days later, the rebels in large numbers besieged and finally captured Lexington, notwithstanding its gallant defence by Colonel Mulligan. Brigadier-General Grant, a name just beginning to come into notice, had been appointed commander of the District of Cairo, had thwarted the plans of the rebel general, Jefferson Thompson, in south-eastern Missouri, occupied Paducah and Smithland, Ky., and early in November, after a careful reconnoissance, had attacked and captured the rebel camp at Belmont, and fought the bloody but indecisive battle at that point.

The Army of the Potomac, now rapidly filling up its numbers under the requisitions of the president, equipped, organized, and disciplined till it was one of the finest armies ever led into the field, whitened all the hills around Washington with its tents. These were the days of " anaconda " strategy. The rebellion was to be surrounded on all sides by our troops, and then, its boundaries being gradually diminished by our contracting lines, at the last the monster was to be crushed into one shapeless mass by the tightening fold of our armies.

The plan is said to have been devised by General Scott, and to have been sanctioned and developed by General McClellan. It was very pretty, and lacked but one element of success — practicability. To have accomplished it would have required at least six millions of men and six billions of money, and even then some weak point would have been found by the enemy. In accordance with this theory, however, expeditions were fitted out for the capture of Forts Hatteras and Clark on the North Carolina coast, and of Forts Beauregard and Walker at Hilton Head, the keys to the fine harbor of Port Royal, and other enterprises were commenced looking to the reduction of Roanoke Island and Newbern, and the capture of New Orleans and its defences. The Hatteras and Hilton Head expeditions both came within the year 1861, and both were successful — the latter owing to the admirable arrangement of Flag-Officer (afterward Rear-Admiral) S. F. Dupont, proving one of the finest naval victories of the war. The war, on the 1st of January, 1862, had raged for nearly nine months, and as yet had made but little impression upon the Southern confederacy. The Union flag floated indeed over a small portion of North and South Carolina; Fort Pickens and Key West were ours; Kentucky was driven from her position of neutrality, though still at several points occupied by the rebels; and Missouri was under Union rule, but sorely harassed by bands of rebel ruffians and guerrillas. The second year of the war was destined to see wider conquests, though not unmingled with serious reverses and disasters. One fold of the anaconda was sweeping southward from St. Louis to the Alleghanies, where an army with its right and left wings three hundred miles asunder pressed the rebel forces before it. The Army of the Western Department, now under command of General Halleck, had its left wing in eastern Kentucky, where the sturdy Thomas swept steadily and grandly onward, defeated Zollicoffer at Camp Wildcat, killed him, and routed most completely his army at Somerset or Mill Spring, and then, his foe having disappeared, hastened to join the centre under Buell. Slow in movement, but an excellent disciplinarian, Buell with the centre had occupied a threatening position toward the rebel stronghold at Bowling Green, where Albert Sydney Johnston, the ablest of the rebel generals, had fortified himself with a large army. Westward still, Grant was moving along the Tennessee and Cumberland Rivers, and preparing under General Halleck's directions one of those flanking movements which have since rendered him so famous, and by which he hoped ere long to render Columbus, Ky., — now strongly fortified and held by a large force under the Bishop-General Polk, — untenable and to compel Johnston to evacuate Bowling Green without a battle. The feat is soon accomplished.

Fort Henry yields on the 6th of February to Flag-Officer Foote's well-directed assault, and on the 16th of the same month Fort Donelson, after a bloody and desperate siege of four days, is "unconditionally surrendered" by General Buckner to General Grant, and fourteen thousand prisoners grace the conqueror's triumph. Clarksville and Nashville were now at the mercy of the Union Army, and Johnston, marching rapidly from Bowling Green, passed through Nashville without stopping, and pushed on to the Mississippi line. While his colleague, the bishop-general, made the best of his way down the river to Island Number Ten, where in a strong position he could for the time defy his pursuers. Grant did not rest upon his laurels. Following his antagonist by way of the Tennessee River, he landed his troops at Pittsburg Landing, near Shiloh Church, about twenty miles from Corinth, a place of great strategic importance, where Johnston was concentrating his forces. General Halleck had ordered Buell and Thomas, the former in advance, to join Grant at this point. The roads were heavy, and the progress of the troops slow. Johnston, a brilliant and skilful soldier, at once saw his opportunity and improved it.

His force, though perhaps not equal to Grant's and Buell's combined, was nearly double that of Grant, and by hurling them upon Grant before his reinforcements came up, he might be able to destroy his army and then to defeat Buell. But the deep mud delayed by a day or more his advance, and Buell was nearer than he supposed. Still, on the first day's attack (Sunday, April 6) the Union troops were in part surprised, and, till near the close of the day, defeated. The greater part of Prentiss' division with its commander were taken prisoners, and the entire army driven out of their camps and toward the river bank. Johnston, the rebel commander, was killed, and Beauregard took his place. Late in the afternoon the tide of battle began to change. The gunboats, coming within range of the enemy, opened upon them with their heavy shells, and Grant's chief of ordnance, gathering the scattered cannon, packed them on a commanding position and commenced so deadly a bombardment at short range that the rebels began to fall back. The gunboats continued their bombardment through the night, and the morning bringing a part of Buell's force, the Union Army assumed the offensive, and by a little afternoon had driven back the rebels and regained the lost ground. The rebels retreated leisurely to Corinth, where they were pursued and besieged till the 30th of May, when Beauregard evacuated it and moved southward.

The battle of Shiloh had been the bloodiest of the war thus far. The bishop-general did not find his stronghold of Island Number Ten impregnable. A canal was cut through a bayou on the west side of the river, by which the gunboats were able to attack it from below, and, New Madrid having been captured by General Pope, the position of the rebels became precarious, and they flitted southward again, leaving, however, their heavy guns and a considerable number of prisoners. Fort Wright was their next halting-place, and ere long they were dispossessed of this, and Memphis was surrendered, the rebel fleet having first been destroyed in a short but sharp naval action. In Arkansas there had been some severe fighting; the Missouri troops, pushing southward to keep up with the sweep of the "anaconda," had encountered the enemy in large force at Pea Ridge, and after a two days' fight, by the gallant conduct of General Sigel the Union troops were victorious, and the rebels driven over the mountains.

The expedition intended for the capture of New Orleans and its defences had wisely been placed under the command of that able and skilful officer Captain (now Vice-Admiral) Farragut, and the coöperating land-force under General Butler. Leaving Fortress Monroe in February, 1862, the expedition was delayed at Ship Island and other points for two months,

and it was not until the 18th of April that it approached Forts Jackson and
St. Philip on the Mississippi, seventy miles below New Orleans. These
forts were works of great strength, and had a large and effective arma-
ment and full garrisons. To make assurance doubly sure, however, the
rebels, to whom the possession of New Orleans was of the greatest importance, had provided against the possibility of a squadron passing the
forts, by stretching a boom and chains across the river, by a large fleet of
gunboats, ironclads, and rams, and by fireships and floating torpedoes
which it was believed would destroy any vessels which might attempt the
hazardous passage. For six days Flag-Officer Farragut bombarded the
forts, and, though he succeeded in doing some damage, there was as yet
no indication of their reduction. He had resolved before, if the bombardment proved unsuccessful, to attempt to force a passage past the
forts and through the obstructions, and thus to reach New Orleans.
The enterprise was one of great hazard. For a distance of nearly a mile
his vessels would be exposed to the secret and terrible fire of the siege-
guns of the forts ; then the chain was to be forced, the fireships, the torpedoes, and the enemy's fleet, nearly equal in numbers to his own, and
several of the vessels ironclad, to be encountered. On the 24th of April,
aided, though some of the time embarrassed, by a fog, the effort was
made, the fire of the forts was encountered without serious injury, the chain
was broken, the fire-rafts and torpedoes destroyed with but slight damage, and the rebel fleet, after a fierce and desperate engagement almost
unparalleled in the history of naval warfare, completely annihilated, thirteen of their gunboats and the ironclad " Manassas " being either burned,
sunk, or destroyed. Of his own squadron, one vessel had been sunk and
three disabled. With the remainder he kept on his way up the river, and
on the 26th summoned New Orleans to surrender. The rebel troops left
the city in haste, and on the 28th it was occupied by Union troops. On
the 29th of April the forts surrendered to Captain (now Rear-Admiral)
Porter. Flag-Officer Farragut ascended the river, captured the forts on its
bank near New Orleans after a brief bombardment, passed the batteries of
Vicksburg, and communicated with Flag-Officer Davis, who had succeeded
the gallant Foote in the command of the upper Mississippi squadron.

On the Atlantic the "anaconda policy" had not worked so well.
Burnside has, indeed, in a brilliant campaign, captured Roanoke Island,
Plymouth, Newbern, Beaufort, and Fort Macon, N.C., and Gilmore had
demonstrated the power of his long-range guns to reduce strong masonry
fortifications, by the capture of Fort Pulaski. But in Virginia matters were
not promising.

The Grand Army of the Potomac lay idly in its camps for four months after its organization was completed. Five and twenty or thirty miles away around the heights of Manassas, the rebel army, far inferior in numbers, in equipments, in ordnance and supplies, had lain through the long winter undisturbed. The new general had ever some excuse ready for declining to move. At length, tired of this constant procrastination, the president took the matter in hand, and issued orders for an advance on the enemy on the 22d of February. When at length the vast army moved forward, the enemy, weary of waiting, had abandoned their camps and moved southward. Marching back to the Potomac, McClellan embarked his main army on transports and sailed for Fortress Monroe. A considerable garrison was left for Washington, a small force in the Shenandoah Valley under General Banks, and one corps under General McDowell stationed near Fredericksburg. Meanwhile, the most remarkable naval conflict of our times had taken place in Hampton Roads. The " Merrimac," one of our own frigates, partially burned at the abandonment of the Gosport Navy Yard, had been raised by the rebels, repaired, and clad with railroad iron. On the 7th of March she came out of Norfolk, destroyed by her ram the " Congress " and " Cumberland," two Union frigates, and attempted to attack the " Minnesota," one of the Union ships of the line, but could not get at her in consequence of the low state of the tide, and during the night lay at anchor ready to renew the destruction of the previous day. But during the night a singular-looking craft, appropriately enough described as resembling a cheese-box on a raft, entered the harbor, and the next morning advanced to give the iron-clad ship battle. In vain the latter exerted all her powers to destroy or escape her little antagonist ; impenetrable to her shots, she is yet nimble enough to sail round her, to throw her huge shells into her portholes whenever they are opened, and to cripple her steering-apparatus ; and at last the monster armored ship, seriously damaged and her commander dangerously wounded, withdrew from the conflict, and a few weeks later was blown up by the rebels to prevent her falling into the hands of the United States authorities. We left the Grand Army on its way to Fortress Monroe. Landing on the peninsula, they soon made their way toward Yorktown, where the rebels, with less than twenty thousand men, occupied some hastily reared works. General McClellan had over one hundred thousand men, and could easily have carried these works by assault, but he preferred to institute a siege ; and General Lee, who was in command, having been largely reinforced, awaited an attack until the 3d of May, when he withdrew to Williamsburg. Hither McClellan followed, fought a battle in which for hours our men

were slaughtered without definite object, and the next morning found that
Lee had left Williamsburg and was moving leisurely toward Richmond.
Thither McClellan pursued as leisurely, digging through the swamps, and
losing more men from the deadly malaria of the Chickahominy marshes
than he would have done in half a dozen battles.

Slowly bridges were thrown across the Chickahominy and a single
division sent across to occupy the ground. The rebels, fully informed of
these movements, sent out a force from Richmond to overwhelm these few
troops, while a rising flood in the Chickahominy would, they reasoned,
prevent their reinforcement. On the first day the Union troops were
defeated and driven back, but, receiving reinforcements, they took the
offensive, and the next day drove the rebels back to within two miles of
Richmond, and could have entered and captured that city had not
McClellan recalled them. For the next twenty-five days General
McClellan continued to fortify the banks of the Chickahominy, his men
meantime falling victims to the malarial fever, till at one time he had
nearly thirty thousand on his sick list — diversifying his labors, meanwhile,
by calling for more men. At this time he had one hundred and fifty-eight
thousand men on his rolls, and one hundred and twenty thousand effectives.
He represented the rebels as having two hundred thousand men, and the
addition of Jackson's corps, which could not, he said, now be prevented,
would increase their force to two hundred and fifty thousand. In fact,
the rebels had fifty thousand men, and when Jackson's corps was added,
less than ninety thousand, and, until they had learned the character of
their foe, were trembling with fear lest we should assault Richmond, which
could not have been held against a resolute attack. After attempting in
vain to throw all the blame of a defeat upon the president or Secretary
Stanton, General McClellan fought two battles, in neither of which did he
employ half his force, and resolved to change his base — or, in plain
English, to raise the siege of Richmond and retreat. This retreat was
conducted under the direct supervision of his subordinate generals, many
of whom by their bravery under such adverse circumstances added to their
reputation. He reached Harrison's Landing, fifteen miles from Richmond, ·
with a loss in killed, wounded, sick, and stragglers of nearly thirty
thousand men. It would still have been possible to have captured Richmond had the Union commander attempted it in earnest, though the diffi-
culty of doing so was immensely increased from his present position ; but
McClellan frittered away the summer in clamoring for more men, and
refused to move without them. The new general-in-chief, General
Halleck, at length recalled the troops to Alexandria and Acquia Creek,

where they were greatly needed. McClellan protested, prayed, and urged further trial, and finding all of no avail, finally, after a fortnight's delay, embarked. Matters were not progressing much more favorably in northern Virginia. General Banks, who had ventured up the Shenandoah Valley in April, driving the rebels before him, was suddenly confronted, early in May, by "Stonewall" Jackson's force, more than quadruple his own, and compelled to retreat, which he did with considerable skill, north of the Potomac. Fremont, now in command of the Mountain Department, and McDowell at Fredericksburg, were summoned to repel his invasion; and his object (of drawing troops away which threatened Richmond from the North) having been accomplished, Jackson in return made a masterly retreat up the Shenandoah Valley, and, after fighting two battles at Cross Keys and Port Republic, made his escape to Gordonsville, and thence, with largely recruited forces, to Richmond, where he arrived in season to harass McClellan's army in its retreat across the peninsula.

It was now resolved to put Fremont's, Banks', and McDowell's commands together under General Pope, as the Army of Virginia, and, threatening Richmond from the north, so distract Lee's attention that it might fall an easy prey to McClellan's attack from the south. General Pope's plans were well arranged, and had he received the coöperation of the Army of the Potomac they could hardly have failed of success. General Pope had advanced toward Richmond, and had crossed the Rappahannock, when he found that Lee, disdaining to notice McClellan's presence at Harrison's Landing or convinced that he had nothing to fear from him, was moving with his whole army, numbering from ninety thousand to one hundred thousand men, upon him. Pope had but forty thousand men, and his only tactics were to fight and fall back till reinforcements could reach him which should make his force equal to that of his adversary. Retreating campaigns are, however, very generally fatal to the morals of an army, unless it is in the highest state of discipline, and it is greatly to General Pope's credit that, fighting at such odds and constantly falling back, unsupported to anything like the extent he should have been by the Army of the Potomac, his brave but half-starved army should have retained to the last its courage, its organization, and its splendid fighting-powers. The battles of this campaign extended from Cedar Mountain by way of Manassas and Centreville almost to the outer defences of Washington itself, and when at last the army of Virginia joined their brethren of the Army of the Potomac within the fortifications around Washington, Lee pressed on into Maryland with the intention of carrying the war into the Northern States, and drawing thence ample supplies for his army.

whom he strongly urged to adopt a system of gradual emancipation, he had fully made up his mind to adopt the measure, and had prepared a proclamation, indicating his intention, early in the summer of 1862, but postponed its publication until it could follow upon the heels of a victory. On the 22d of September, 1862, he issued his proclamation, announcing that on the first day of January, 1863, he should proclaim all the slaves in States and parts of States which were then insurgent free, and that he pledged the power of the government to effect and maintain their freedom.

The new year (1863) dawned upon the consummation of this act of emancipation. It was hailed by the colored race with extravagant joy, while the rebels, who saw in it the presage of their downfall, were greatly exasperated, and made abundant threats and passed acts of retaliation. The year was, however, one of general prosperity to the Union cause. The disasters were few and the successes many. Numerous regiments of colored troops were enlisted in the service of the Union, and on many battle-fields proved their courage and ability. In the East, after a brief period, Hooker succeeded Burnside in command of the Army of the Potomac, and attempted to turn Lee's left flank at Chancellorsville, sending, meantime, a cavalry force to cut his communications. Lee, fully master of the situation, met Hooker's movement by a counter flank, sending "Stonewall" Jackson to strike and roll up Hooker's right, which he accomplished, partly from a want of watchfulness on the part of the Union troops, and partly from the panic with which his sudden attack struck a part of the Eleventh Corps. The battle raged fiercely that night and the next morning, and Hooker's troops were not only forced back, but crowded northward toward the fords of the Rappahannock. Sedgwick's corps, which had been ordered to take Fredericksburg, and had accomplished its work after a severe battle, pressing westward to join the rest of the army, encountered the whole of Lee's army instead, which had passed Hooker, and, while his forces lay still in their camps, were fighting all day long with Sedgwick's single corps of brave men. Hooker finally recrossed the Rappahannock without having accomplished his object, but with heavy losses in men and artillery. Lee, emboldened by the supposed demoralization of Hooker's army, and not deterred by the ill success of his former inroad into the Northern States, started early in June for a new and more extensive expedition. Hooker followed and occupied interior lines, crowding Lee's army westward by means of his cavalry, beyond the Bull Run Mountains, and compelling him to cross the Potomac higher up than he liked. The last days of June indicated by the approaching columns of

the two armies that the great conflict would take place at or near Gettysburg, Penn., and hither the army of the Potomac, under its new commander, General Meade (General Hooker having been relieved), hastened,
and for three days battle raged as never before on this continent. The
Union army, partially defeated the first day, gained and held the strong
positions of Cemetery Hill, Round Top, and Little Round Top, and repulsed all the assaults of the enemy with a most fearful slaughter, till at
last, his best troops slain, some of his ablest generals killed and wounded,
one-third of his army put *hors de combat*, and his ammunition nearly ex-
pended, he began to move for the Potomac.

Meade's pursuit was not so active and vigilant as it should have been,
or he might have compelled the surrender of Lee's army; but he had un-
doubtedly achieved a great victory. Lee escaped to the Rapidan, and
thither Meade followed; and except an unsuccessful attempt of the latter to
penetrate between the wings of Lee's army in the autumn, there was no
further movement of the two armies during the year. Charleston must
be captured; and while an attack on its outer defences in the summer of
1862 had proved abortive, and a naval assault under Rear-Admiral Dupont
in April had been unavailing, the government and the nation were not
satisfied. General Gilmore, the hero of Fort Pulaski, was put in command
of the land forces, and Rear-Admiral Dahlgren of the naval force. General
Gilmore chose Morris Island as the base of his operations. The lower
portion of the island was occupied; the strong earthwork, Fort Wagner,
twice assaulted with fearful loss, and finally captured by siege operations;
Fort Sumter bombarded till it was a shapeless mass of ruins; and Charleston shelled till its entire lower town became uninhabitable. In the
Gulf, Galveston had been captured by a portion of Rear-Admiral Farragut's squadron, only to be held, however, for a few weeks, when by a
treacherous attack the rebels regained possession, captured the " Harriet
Lane," and caused the destruction of the " Westfield." In this unfortunate
affair the gallant Renshaw, Wainwright, Lee, and Zimmerman, officers of
the United States Navy, sacrificed their lives. On the Mississippi, General Grant, after trying in vain to capture Vicksburg from the north and
northwest, sent several of the gunboats, and a number of transports passed
the batteries in safety, and, marching his troops down the west side of the
Mississippi, crossed at Bruinsburg, thirty miles below Vicksburg, and,
moving north-eastward, fought six battles in seventeen days, captured
Jackson, the capital of the State, and sat down before Vicksburg, which he
now completely invested, on the 18th of May. After two assaults, neither
of them productive of much advantage, he proceeded with a regular system

of approaches, till the rebels surrendered on the 4th of July. The trophies of this victory were thirty-one thousand prisoners and over four hundred guns. Port Hudson, below, was surrendered four days later, and the Mississippi flowed untrammelled to the sea. Rosecrans, early in June, had commenced moving forward to press Bragg farther south, making Chattanooga his objective. Driving him from Tullahoma, the advance on Chattanooga was necessarily slow, as the railroads and bridges were to be reconstructed with a view to permanence, that his supplies from his primary and secondary bases — Louisville and Nashville — might be safely and rapidly transmitted. It was, as we have said, his intention to occupy Chattanooga, but to carry that important point by direct attack would have required the sacrifice of more men than he could spare, and he accordingly prepared to accomplish it by a movement by the right flank, sending his *corps d'armee* to cross Lookout Mountain at different passes miles below Chattanooga, and thus threatening his communications with lower Georgia. The expected result followed. Chattanooga was evacuated, and occupied by a small Union force ; but Bragg, having at this time received large reinforcements, resolved to regain that city, and, striking Rosecrans before his three corps could unite, to defeat him in detail. By great exertion Rosecrans was able to effect a junction of his army corps, and in the great battle of Chickamauga, his first day's fighting, though severe, was without result. The second day, by an unfortunate misunderstanding of an order, a gap was left in the Union lines, and about one-third of the army, including General Rosecrans himself and two of the corps commanders, McCook and Crittenden, were swept back and were unable to force their way through to the remainder of the army. Bragg now supposed he had an easy victory before him, but the sturdy Thomas won for himself new honors. Setting his back to the mountains, the " Rock of Chickamauga," as he has been appropriately named, fought it out with a foe five times his numbers, and when the enemy rolled up toward his little army for the last time, hurled upon them Steedman's fresh division, and drove them back, defeated and sullen at the loss of their expected prey.

Almost simultaneously with this movement, Burnside had occupied Knoxville and captured Cumberland Gap, and Tennessee was again in possession of the United States. But the possession of Chattanooga was not to be maintained without a further struggle. Bragg was still further reinforced, and Hooker, Sherman, Blair, and Howard were sent to reinforce the Army of the Cumberland ; Rosecrans was relieved and Thomas put in his place, and Grant made the commander of the whole Western Division.

Embarrassed at first by the want of supplies, as the rebels held a part of the railroad and commanded a portion of the river, they were soon relieved by the manœuvres of Grant and the battle of Wauhatchie, which secured the command of the river. When Bragg finally announced his determination to bombard the city, having sent off at the same time twenty thousand of his men to besiege Knoxville, Grant replied by sending Hooker to drive him from Lookout Mountain, and fight that battle "above the clouds" which will be famous in history, detaching a cavalry force to cut the railroad lines and prevent the return of the men who had gone to Knoxville, directing Sherman to demonstrate persistently and heavily upon Fort Buckner, while he hurled Gordon Granger's corps upon Fort Bragg, and Hooker's upon Fort Breckinridge. Bragg was routed with terrible loss of men and guns, and his demoralized army driven beyond Mission Ridge and Pigeon Mountain to the Chattoogata or Rocky-Faced Ridge.

In 1864 new and grander combinations were made for the overthrow of the rebellion. Inefficient officers were weeded out from all positions, high or low, and the administration exhibited more decidedly than before its determination to press the war to a speedy conclusion. Sherman's raid into central Mississippi and Alabama, with twenty thousand men, was of more value for the terror it carried into the hearts of the rebel population than for any other result. The Red River expedition, a miserable and disastrous failure, and the battle of Chester, only less miserable and disastrous because fewer troops were engaged, were the last vestiges of the "anaconda" system. Henceforth there were but two grand centres of military authority, the Lieutenant-General Ulysses S. Grant, General-in-Chief, but personally commanding the Division of the East, and Major-General Sherman, commanding the Division of the Mississippi; and these two worked together with a perfect unity of purpose. Richmond, or rather Lee's army, Atlanta, or Johnston's army, were the objectives of each.

Early in May the grand movements commenced. Grant, with nearly two hundred thousand men under his control in the three armies of the Potomac, the James, and West Virginia, moved forward in concert toward Richmond; and in a series of battles unequalled in modern history for their terrible destruction of human life — battles which will make the names of Wilderness, Spottsylvania, Hanover, Court House, Cold Harbor, Mechanicsville, and Chickahominy memorable in all the future — drove Lee back to Richmond; then swinging his troops across the James laid siege to Petersburg, and by rapid and heavy blows — now upon the de-

fences of Richmond, anon upon the Weldon Railroad, mining the rebel
fortifications of Petersburg, throwing his troops across Hatcher's Run to
break the South side Railroad, sending his cavalry to cut the communications of the rebel capital — kept the rebel commander constantly on the
alert, and held his forces as in a vise at this point.   In sheer desperation,
Lee attempted another expedition, with his irregular and a few regular
troops, into Maryland and Pennsylvania; but Early, its commander,
though he plundered several towns and burned one, soon found his
master in the fighting cavalry general, Philip Sheridan, whom Grant
sent to take care of him; defeated at Opequan Creek and "sent whirl-
ing" through Winchester; routed from Fisher's Hill and driven in hot
haste and thorough disorder up the valley, till his men were fain to hide
in the mountains; and when, reinforced, he again ventured to seek his
foe, driven back in disgrace; and when, on a third effort, which promised
to be successful, he had, in Sheridan's absence, flanked his position and
driven his army several miles, how completely were the tables turned at
Sheridan's sudden appearance !   Driven back at full speed twenty-six miles
in a single night, his cannon left behind, and the line of his flight marked
at almost every step by the muskets, knapsacks, blankets, and coats his
men had thrown away, poor Early was glad, henceforth, to keep well out
of Sheridan's reach.   Fierce and bloody battles were not uncommon between the two resolute and well-matched antagonists, Lee and Grant; but
while the latter often lost the most men, he gained something with each
battle, and at length drew his lines so closely that the pressure began to
be intolerable. In January, 1865, Lee apprised Jefferson Davis that without
some great changes he could not hold out six months longer. After two
severe battles on the 6th of February and the 25th of March, 1865, the
final struggle came; and after a five days' contest, in which a great cavalry
battle was fought at Dinwiddie Court House, and sharp and severe actions
near Hatcher's Run, at Five Forks, and around the fortifications of Petersburg, the Southside Railroad was broken, the outer works at Petersburg
captured, and Petersburg and Richmond evacuated.   Six days later, and
after battles at Deatonsville, Farmville, and Appomattox Station, Lee and
his army surrendered.

Sherman's career was more brilliant, though perhaps not more certain
of eventual success.   Leaving Chattanooga on the 7th of May, 1864, and
moving mostly by the right flank, he drove Johnston successively from
Dalton, Resaca, Kingston, Dallas, Great and Little Kenesaw Mountains,
(an assault on the rebel position on the former mountain proving the
greatest disaster of the campaign), Allatoona Pass, Marietta, and De-

catur; and Johnston, having been superseded by Hood, fought three sharp battles before Atlanta, in all of which Hood lost very heavily. After besieging Atlanta in vain for some time, he boldly raised the siege, and, moving twenty miles below, broke up Hood's communications, fought and defeated two of his army corps at Jonesboro, and compelled the evacuation of Atlanta. Taking possession of that city, he sent off the inhabitants and accumulated stores there for further movements. Hood attempted to cut his communications between Atlanta and Chattanooga, and boasted of his intention to regain possession of Tennessee. Sherman followed him along the Chattanooga and Atlanta Railroad, fought and repulsed him at Allatoona Pass, drove him through Pigeon Mountain and westward to Gaylesville, Ala., and then, having assigned two corps of his own army to General Thomas and directed other outlying divisions to move toward Nashville, he gave him general instructions to take care of Hood, and with the four remaining infantry corps and a well-appointed cavalry force, turned his face southward, destroyed the railroad from Dalton to Atlanta, burned the public storehouses at Atlanta, and on the 14th of November, with an army of sixty thousand men, abandoned his base and struck out boldly for Savannah, nearly three hundred miles distant. By a skilful handling of his troops, now threatening one point and now another, he managed to prevent any considerable gathering of the enemy in his track, and, with nothing more than a few skirmishes, captured Millidgeville, reached the vicinity of Savannah, and carried Fort McAllister by assault on the 14th of December. On the 20th Hardee evacuated Savannah, and Sherman entered it the next day. Meantime Hood, finding that Sherman had moved toward Savannah, left his camp in Alabama and marched northward, intent upon again occupying Tennessee. General Schofield, who was at Pulaski, had orders to fight him moderately and lure him on northward, but to delay his progress till General Thomas' reinforcements could come up; he performed this difficult task with extraordinary skill, falling back, fighting all the way from Pulaski to Columbia, from Columbia to the north bank of Duck River, and thence by a forced march to Franklin. At Franklin a severe battle was fought, on the 3d of November; Schofield's army, though greatly inferior in numbers, being behind breastworks and inflicting terrible punishment on the rebels. In this battle Hood lost thirteen generals. Falling back again to Nashville, the rebel general followed, and attempted to reduce Nashville by besieging it on the side; but after a fortnight General Thomas, sallying forth with his army, crushed one wing of Hood's army and drove him back two or three miles the first day, and renewing the attack on the following day routed him completely, and pursuing him relentlessly for two weeks, only ceased when his entire army, except a rear-guard of about four thousand, was a demoralized and unarmed mob.

Having thus so completely broken up Hood's fine army that it was no longer to be regarded as an organized force, General Thomas increased his cavalry force and sent one large division, under General Stoneman, eastward into southwestern Virginia and North Carolina; three divisions or about fifteen thousand mounted men southward, under General Wilson, into Alabama and Georgia; one corps of infantry to Mobile; and another eastward to Wilmington. General Sherman remained about one month in Savannah and its vicinity, and then moved forward on the third stage of the "great march."

His objective this time was Goldsboro. N.C. more than four hundred miles distant. His army, marching in two columns and veiled on either wing by Kilpatrick's cavalry, cut a swarth of forty miles in width through the heart of South and North Carolina, taking possession of Orangeburg, Columbia, Winnsboro, Cheraw, Fayetteville, and Goldsboro, and compelling the rebels to evacuate Charleston, which General Gilmore entered on the 18th of February, and other important points on the seaboard. In all this route he fought but two battles, one at Averysboro, the other at Bentonville, N.C., in both of which he defeated Johnston. Arrived at Goldsboro, he remained there for a little more than two weeks refitting his army. On the 19th of June, 1864, off Cherbourg, France, occurred a naval battle between the United States sloop of war "Kearsage," Captain Winslow, and the Anglo-rebel privateer, the "Alabama," which for two years had committed terrible ravages among the merchant vessels of the United States. The commander of the "Alabama" was the challenger; but after a severe fight of about an hour, the "Alabama" was compelled to surrender, and sunk soon after; about thirty of her crew were drowned, about seventy were picked up by the boats of the "Kearsage," and the remainder, including the rebel commander, were rescued by the "Deerhound," an English yacht which seemed to act as tender for the "Alabama," and most dishonorably carried them to the English shore and set them at liberty.

General Grant, desirous of checking the blockade-running and of crippling Lee's resources, had sent in December a joint land and naval force to reduce Fort Fisher, a strong earthwork commanding the entrance to Wilmington harbor. The first expedition had proved a failure, but a second had been promptly fitted out. — the land forces under General

Terry, the naval as before under Rear-Admiral Porter, —and after a most desperate and persistent assault of six hours the fort was captured and the works adjacent surrendered.   After a brief period of rest General Terry moved forward to carry the other forts and batteries defending the harbor, and General Schofield and his corps were brought from Nashville to assist in the work.   On the 21st of February, Wilmington was evacuated after some hard fighting, and on the 22d it was occupied by Schofield's and Terry's troops.   These two corps now moved forward through Kinston, where they had a severe battle, to Goldsboro, to join Sherman.   On the 10th of April Sherman again moved on with his army in pursuit of Johnston, driving him from Southfield on the 11th and from Raleigh on the 13th.   Here the news of Lee's surrender reached them, and the Union troops pushed forward with new ardor to conquer Johnston's army also. General Johnston, seeing escape to be hopeless, now made overtures for surrender, but desired somewhat different terms from those accorded to Lee, and proposed to surrender the entire rebel armies in the field.   A memorandum was drawn up by Johnston and Sherman and sent to Washington for sanction, but was unanimously disapproved by the president and cabinet, General Grant concurring.   The lieutenant-general carried the intelligence of its rejection to General Sherman, and within twenty-four hours General Johnston desired another interview and surrendered on the same terms accorded to General Lee.

The assassination of the president, which occurred on the 14th of April, did not, as it was feared it might, delay the approach of peace ; for the hopelessness of the struggle being apparent, the rebel commanders were everywhere ready to lay down their arms.   On the 5th of August, 1864, the Forts Morgan, Powell, and Gaines, at the entrance to Mobile harbor, had been attacked by a combined force under General Canby and Rear-Admiral Farragut, and after a desperate naval battle in which the iron-clad ram "Tennessee," the *chef-d'œuvre* of the rebel armored ships, was captured and two others of their gunboats destroyed, the forts were one after another reduced, till on the 23d of August the last surrendered. Other operations, and the necessity for the employment of troops elsewhere, delayed the siege of the city of Mobile until March, 1865, when, a substantial force having been assembled on the coast, a combined naval and land attack was made, and the formidable defences of the city were carried one after another, and the city surrendered on the 11th of April. The hundreds of torpedoes with which the bay was planted caused the destruction of two iron-clads and four other vessels of the United States Navy.

The surrender of Mobile was soon followed by the surrender of General Dick Taylor and his army, on the same terms which had been accorded to Lee and Johnston, and the giving up of the rebel navy on the waters of Alabama. General Wilson, with his magnificent cavalry corps, had swept through central Alabama and Georgia, capturing Selma, Montgomery, West Point, Columbus, and Macon; and Stoneman, moving eastward from Knoxville, had reached Salisbury, infamous as one of the prison-pens of our brave soldiers; and the two cavalry generals were now moving toward each other in search of the fugitive rebel, President Jefferson Davis. A detachment of Wilson's corps arrested him on the 10th of May, 1865, at Irwinville, Georgia, in the act of attempting to escape in feminine garb. The arch traitor in custody, there remained no more rebels in arms except Kirby Smith's force in Texas, which also surrendered on the 26th of May.

Thus ended the rebellion and the war for the restoration of the Union. It had cost more than half a million of lives, and in the debts of the two sections and the destruction of property and values not less than eight thousand millions of money; but fearful as its expense had been, it is worth all it has cost. Slavery has been destroyed, the State Rights heresy effectually overthrown, and the power of the nation to maintain its integrity in spite of domestic treason or foreign interference fully demonstated. Henceforth we are one people — one in purpose and aim, one in our hopes for the present and our aspirations for the future. There may and will be jealousies and prejudices to be overcome; bitterness will rankle in some hearts perhaps during the lifetime of the present generation; but henceforth the banner of the free shall float over an undivided, free, happy, and prosperous land; and the vast resources, still but half developed, which will draw to our shores in rapidly increasing numbers the oppressed of all nations, will soon lighten our burdens, and cause the war to be remembered only for the patriotism it developed and the blessings it has secured to us.

LIBBY PRISON.

BY COMRADE NELSON MONROE.

FROM the corner of a dingy brick building in one of the streets of Richmond, Va., there could have been seen, at the breaking out of the rebellion in 1861, a small sign, which told to the passer-by that " Libby & Son, Ship Chandlers and Grocers," had invited their patrons to this point, as the one where their business was conducted, and where those must repair who were interested in bargains particularly associated with their vocation. It was not of sufficient importance in time of peace to obtain a wide celebrity, neither were the owners thereof so distinguished as to be of great notoriety; but as the inauguration of war has inducted many into office who were hitherto obscure and unknown, so the contingencies of our civil strife have opened this place to the public gaze and made it *famous*, or rather *in*famous, before the world, beside conferring a lustreless fame upon the proprietors. The very name of Libby has become synonymous with that of *terror*; it carries tyranny and oppression in its simple sound. The soldier who is taken prisoner in Virginia vales is at once haunted with visions of this darksome den, and shrinks from entering a place so full of bitter experiences as that is known to be.

Fierce hate and revenge reigned supreme there, and consequently there was wrought out a system of discipline which produced a condition such as we might expect when the discordant elements of being rage unchecked; and we are not surprised to find the culmination reached in almost fiendish expression. Thousands who have been in Libby Prison will rehearse the story of their misery, want, and woe to others; these will pass them along to other listeners still, so that the echo will scarcely die out at the remotest period of the present generation. Households, in coming time, will gather about the fireside and talk of their friends and ancestors who ended their days in so much wretchedness because of their attachment to the Union, and in proportion as their bravery and heroism, their courage and constancy, are admired will the malice and fury of their persecutors be condemned.

It may be, and probably is, one of the essentials of war that places be provided for the confinement of prisoners : but they do not necessarily include every species of torment which the human mind is capable of conceiving. They should not naturally presuppose the absence of all humanity and the annihilation of every condition of comfortable existence, as they have seemed to in almost every part of the South where the Confederate authorities existed.

Their treatment of prisoners was very abusive, kicking them, and never speaking of one only in the most opprobrious terms.

The nights were very cold, and, there being nothing but gratings in the windows, the men were obliged to walk all night long to keep from freezing, and if they could meet the friendly embrace of slumber at all, it was during the day, when the sun would shed its kindly beams upon them, and so imparting sufficient warmth to their bodies to keep them from shivering.

You have no idea of their utter destitution when you listen to the statement they make respecting the manner of their obtaining the food which they must have in some way or perish.

I have seen men draw their bean-soup in their *shoes* for the want of a cup, plate, or anything of the kind to put it in. And what seemed worse than all the rest was the almost satanic rule that if a man was caught resting his eye upon the glad scenes of nature through a window he must be quickly translated from earth by the ball of a musket. The whole thing is arbitrary in the extreme ; but we could expect little else under the very shadow of the Confederate capitol, where the original framers of secession go in and out, seeking to form a dynasty, though it be founded in the tears and blood, the cries and groans, of their fellow-men. Of the numbers who have been admitted within the walls of the Libby Building we can scarcely speak, for the multitudes have been conveyed thither temporarily, to remain only until such time as they could be transported to other places. Very many thousands have found a transient home here, and their united testimony is the same.

It was three stories high, and eighty feet in width, and a hundred and ten feet in depth. In front, the first story was on a level with the street, allowing space for a tier of dungeons under the sidewalk ; but in the rear the land sloped away till the basement floor rose above the ground. Its unpainted walls were scorched to a rusty brown, and its sunken doors and low windows, filled here and there with a dusky pane, were cobwebbed and weather-stained, giving the whole building a most uninviting and desolate appearance.

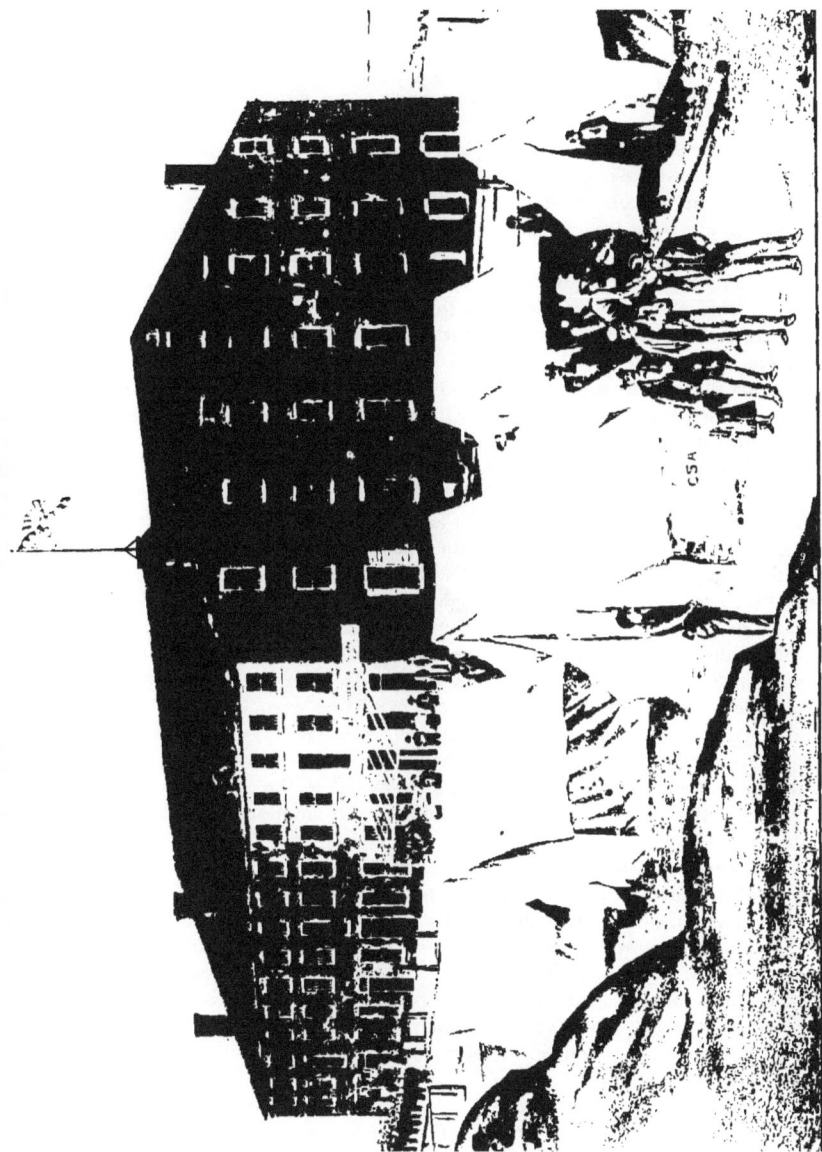

LIBBY PRISON.

As it appeared in 1861 and 1866.

Upon passing inside, we entered a room about forty feet wide and a hundred feet deep, with bare brick walls, a rough plank floor, and narrow, dingy windows, to whose sash only a few broken panes were clinging. A row of tin wash-basins, and a wooden trough, which served as a bathing-tub, were at one end of it, and a half-dozen cheap stools and hard-bottomed chairs were littered about the floor, but it had no other furniture : and this room, with five others of similar size and appointments, and two basements floored with earth and filled with *débris*, composed the famous Libby Prison, in which for months together thousands of the best and bravest men that ever went into battle have been allowed to rot and to starve.

From the time the war began, twelve and sometimes thirteen hundred of our officers and men were hived within those half-dozen desolate rooms and filthy cellars, with a space of only ten feet by two allotted to each for all the purposes of living.

Overrun with vermin, perishing with cold, breathing a stifled, tainted atmosphere, no space allowed them for rest by day, and lying down at night "wormed and dovetailed together like fish in a basket," their daily rations only two ounces of stale beef and a small lump of hard corn-bread, and their lives the forfeit if they caught but one streak of God's blue sky through those filthy windows,* — they have endured all these horrors in the middle passage. My soul sickened as I looked upon the scene of their wretchedness. If the liberty we were fighting for were not worth even so terrible a price, if it were not cheaply purchased even with the blood and agony of the many brave and true souls who have gone into that foul den only to die or to come out the shadows of men,—living ghosts, condemned to walk the night and to fade away before the breaking of the great day that is coming,— who would not cry out for peace, for peace on any terms ?

We need no other proof of the true nobleness of soul in the young men of our country than the voices which come ever and anon from these forbidding prison-places, telling us of a quenchless love for the cause of right ; of a devotion and fervor that know no abatement, and a willingness to do and to dare, to suffer and to die, that the tyrant of oppression may be crushed, and the glad hosannas of Freedom ring through the land and reverberate among the hills : that we may have not a "circle within a circle," but one that is continuous, unbroken, clasping in its mighty embrace a free, happy, and united people.

---

* See poem, "'The Dead Line' at Libby Prison."

"THE DEAD LINE" AT LIBBY PRISON.

FROM his box the rebel soldier watched his sad and weary foe,
While the noon in solemn silence seemed unwilling far to go,
As if it did wish to whisper to the sad and weary there,
How it smiled o'er Western prairies and New England valleys fair;
And the starving son looked on it, and the weeping mother too,
One at home and one in prison, but their hearts together drew.
And the pining husband saw it, and his fond and loving wife,
One looked from her chamber sleepless, one was trying to hold life.
Oh! the moon was brightly beaming, as it on its way did roam,
And it lit the soldier's prison and it lit his far-off home.
Wife and mother asked beneath it, Where's my husband and my boy?
Months have passed since I heard from them, and shall time my hopes
    destroy?
Son and husband asked beneath it, Where's the mother and the wife?
Do they know how now I suffer, how I'm loth to part with life?
Do they know the peril of it, if we leave the heated clime,
And without a moment's warning put our feet on the Dead Line?

Distant friend, how we have suffered for the want of food and clothes,
How we've daily pined with hunger, but the God of Heaven knows,
And how we have had no shelter from the sun and from the storm.
Ah! it sent to yonder graveyard many a once stout, noble form.
Ah! we've seen the light of hoping leaving many a once bright eye,
And we've seen the strong and robust turn to skeletons and die,
And we knew why they were numbered with the cold and silent dead
Was because they had no shelter, and ate filth instead of bread;
And we heard how distant fond ones, from the golden State of Maine,
Sent us blankets to wrap round us, sent us food life to sustain,
But the minions of Jeff Davis robbed the starving prisoners there,
While their chivalry they boasted, and their leader formed a prayer.
'Twas a prayer for aid from Heaven on the traitors' cherished plans,
As if God himself could sanction all the ways they murdered man,
As if He could look with favor on the fiends who there combine
To cause famine and exposure to force some to the Dead Line.

And why should the traitor soldier be too cautious ere he fires?
And why should he loudly challenge, when so glowing his desires?
And why would he not aim steady when he gets a leader's praise,
And if thus he shoots a Yankee, has a furlough thirty days?
Other nights they may be dismal, and the line may pass from view;
Still the bloodhounds, trained to watching, eye the weak and helpless too;
And the sentinels are knowing that his food has made him so,
That his stomach is disordered, and his face portrays his woe;
And for him they have no pity, for their hearts like rivers freeze,
Though he suffers from starvation and the inroads of disease.
Still the glimmering hope is cherished, 'mid the many dangers there,
That again he may be knowing a fond wife or mother's care.
And he ponders as he wanders, Nature does assert its right,
And each sentinel well knoweth the poor prisoner's dreadful plight,
But, oh! nothing say unto him, from him hide not the marked place,
For you'll never get a furlough, if you warn him from the line.

Hark! There is a scream of terror, traitor minions heed it not,
For it's not of much importance, but a Yankee soldier's shot.
Not a fence was there to warn him, and the marks were hard to see,
But a " Reb " has got a furlough and a prisoner's soul set free.
There's another squad of Yankees waiting and watching there.
How we wish when we are guarding some would try to cross the line.
'Tis a wonder they don't try it when they have to suffer so;
And it is our leader's study how to starve or freeze each foe,
So that he may ne'er be useful in the foeman's ranks again;
And the pale and tottering " Yankees " tell the hope is not in vain;
While they from their Northern prisons stouter send our prisoners back,
With no crushed hopes in their bosoms and no bloodhounds on their track;
And to keep their hard-earned money they did not in vain beseech,
Nor when wishing for an apple pay a dollar bill for each;
And no Federal had a furlough to make hopes the brighter shine,
Till he shot a helpless foeman full five feet from the Dead Line.

Who'll forget the rude old wagons in which they our dead conveyed,
And the loathsome, shabby manner in which our brothers there were laid?
Who'll forget the same rude wagons, in which they conveyed our dead,
After served another purpose — that of bringing us our bread,
That of bringing us our " corn-cob," which they cruelly called meal,
While the life-blood from the soldiers it would like a robber steal?

Who'll forget the putrid " beef-steaks," twenty men on one to dine,
Peas in which huge worms were gathered as if drawn in battle line?
Who'll forget the black swamp-water and the crocodiles near by?
Who'll forget the chains so heavy in which foes let prisoners die?
Who'll forget the smoky pine-fires round which clustered "heart-sick bands,
Speaking of the friends they treasured, while they looked like "contrabands"?
Who'll forget the rampant villains saying we deserved our lot,
And the "unknown" who were buried in the trench — a fearful spot?
Who'll forget the countless horrors — there's no book the tenth could tell,
For Libby Prison nothing lacketh to make it the Earthly Hell.   .

See the graveyard yonder swelling with the prisoners paroled.
Let us trust their noble spirits have gone to their Saviour's fold.
Ah! how many forms were murdered in a cold and shocking way—
Can their treatment be forgotten while our souls are in this clay?
It needs something more than human to forget what brave men bore,
To forget the graveyard swelling and the hearts that suffered sore,
To forget the noble comrades who did perish midst our foes,
For the want of food and shelter, while the rebels stole their clothes.
To forget the horrid treatment mortal man must feel to know.
There's no human comprehension that can realize the woe;
But be tried as foes have tried us, fearing that we would survive,
And you wonder that a mortal left that Earthly Hell alive.
There were many, many spirits left Libby Prison and took flight,
As if they had wings of angels, to the land of life and light;
Many who were often longing they could leave the accursed place,
And the angels bade them welcome, far outside of the Dead Line.

And now, comrades, this is what we have done; and thirty years have passed and gone.

Our friendship with each other, in Fraternity, Charity, and Loyalty, has with those years stronger grown; and as we look back upon the past, and think of our comrades who have answered the final roll-call we wonder why it was not our fate to be called from that Earthly Hell (Libby Prison). Who can answer? But, comrades, as we have been spared this, the Grand Army Button, to wear, let us wear it as a "Souvenir" (as it is), in remembrance of the past, and thank God that we did not approach too near the Dead Line.